Great Meals in Minutes was created by
Rebus, Inc.
and published by Time-Life Books.

Rebus, Inc.

Publisher: Rodney Friedman
Editorial Director: Shirley Tomkievicz

Editor: Marya Dalrymple
Art Director: Ronald Gross
Managing Editor: Brenda Goldberg
Senior Editor: Cara De Silva
Food Editor and Food Stylist: Grace Young
Photographer: Steven Mays
Prop Stylist: Cathryn Schwing
Staff Writer: Alexandra Greeley
Associate Editors: Ann Harvey, Barbara
Benton
Assistant Editor: Bonnie J. Slotnick
Assistant Food Stylist: Nancy Leland
Thompson
Recipe Tester: Gina Palombi Barclay
Production Assistant: Lorna Bieber

For information about any Time-Life book,
please write:
Reader Information
Time-Life Books
541 North Fairbanks Court
Chicago, Illinois 60611
Library of Congress Cataloging in Publication Data
Egg & cheese menus.
  (Great meals in minutes)
  Includes index.
  1. Cookery (Eggs) 2. Cookery (Cheese)
  3. Menus. 4. Cooks—Biography.
I. Time-Life Books. II. Title:
Egg and cheese menus. III. Series.
TX745.E4 1984   641.6'73 84-16313
ISBN 0-86706-195-2 (lib. bdg.)
ISBN 0-86706-194-4 (retail ed.)

Time-Life Books Inc.
is a wholly owned subsidiary of
Time Incorporated

Founder: Henry R. Luce 1898–1967
Editor-in-Chief: Henry Anatole Grunwald
President: J. Richard Munro
Chairman of the Board: Ralph P. Davidson
Corporate Editor: Jason McManus
Group Vice President, Books: Reginald K.
Brack Jr.

Time-Life Books Inc.

Editor: George Constable
Executive Editor: George Daniels
Director of Design: Louis Klein
Board of Editors: Roberta Conlan,
Ellen Phillips, Gerry Schremp, Gerald
Simons, Rosalind Stubenberg, Kit van
Tulleken, Henry Woodhead
Editorial General Manager: Neal Goff
Director of Research: Phyllis K. Wise
Director of Photography: John Conrad Weiser

President: Reginald K. Brack Jr.
Senior Vice President: William Henry
Vice Presidents: George Artandi, Stephen L.
Bair, Robert A. Ellis, Juanita T. James,
Christopher T. Linen, James L. Mercer,
Joanne A. Pello, Paul R. Stewart

Editorial Operations
Design: Ellen Robling (assistant director)
Copy Room: Diane Ullius
Production: Ann B. Landry (director), Celia
Beattie
Quality Control: James J. Cox (director), Sally
Collins
Library: Louise D. Forstall

SERIES CONSULTANT
Margaret E. Happel is the author of *Ladies
Home Journal Adventures in Cooking*,
*Ladies Home Journal Handbook of Holiday
Cuisine*, and other best-selling cookbooks, as
well as the translator and adapter of Rebecca
Hsu Hiu Min's *Delights of Chinese Cooking*.
A food consultant based in New York City,
she has been director of the food department
of *Good Housekeeping* and editor of
American Home magazine.

WINE CONSULTANT
Tom Maresca combines a full-time career
teaching English literature with writing
about and consuming fine wines. He is now
at work on *The Wine Case Book*, which
explains the techniques of wine tasting.

Cover: Douglas Oaks's baked eggs in Idaho
potatoes, honey-glazed Brussels sprouts with
walnuts, and tomatoes vinaigrette. See pages
20–21.

Great Meals
IN MINUTES

EGG & CHEESE
MENUS

TIME
LIFE
BOOKS

TIME-LIFE BOOKS, ALEXANDRIA, VIRGINIA

Contents

Meet the Cooks

DOUGLAS OAKS

Certified as an executive chef and culinary educator by the American Culinary Federation, Douglas Oaks has received numerous cooking awards, including top prizes in the National Culinary Competition held annually in Chicago. He has trained in restaurants in Minneapolis and St. Paul and studied cooking abroad. Currently, he is executive chef at Litton Microwave Cooking.

COPELAND MARKS

Born and educated in Vermont, Copeland Marks pursues two careers. As a textile collector and importer, he travels extensively in Asia and Central America, and he researches and writes about the foods he encounters while traveling. He is the author of *The Indonesian Kitchen* and has recently completed cookbooks on Guatemalan, Mayan, and Central American foods; on Tibetan cooking; and on the cuisine of the Jewish community in Calcutta. He regularly contributes articles to food magazines.

ANN CASHION

Born in Jackson, Mississippi, Ann Cashion has worked in bakeries and restaurants in and around San Francisco, where she opened the Oh-la-la Bakery in 1982. Previously, she had been a cook at Trattoria Ricchi, a Tuscan restaurant outside Florence, Italy. She now creates menus and cooks at Restaurant Nora in Washington, D.C.

HOWARD HELMER AND ARLENE WANDERMAN

Howard Helmer is the eastern representative for the American Egg Board and the author of *The Forty-Second Omelet, Guaranteed!* Arlene Wanderman has worked as a metabolic research dietician at various New York hospitals and as the food and equipment editor for *Ladies' Home Journal.* Together they manage Food Communications, Inc., a public relations firm.

PENELOPE CASAS

Penelope Casas lived in Spain for many years and visits Spain annually to add to her collection of regional recipes. She currently teaches at the New York Cooking Center, lectures on Spanish cuisine at New York University, and has written about travel and food for *Vogue, Cuisine,* and *Bon Appétit.* She is the author of *The Food and Wines of Spain,* which received the 1983 Spanish national gastronomy prize.

JEAN ANDERSON

A native of Raleigh, North Carolina, Jean Anderson first cooked at the age of five, beginning a life-long interest in food. After earning a B.S. in Food and Nutrition at Cornell University and a graduate degree in journalism at Columbia University, she became a food editor of *Ladies' Home Journal* as well as a contributing editor of *Family Circle.* Now a freelance photojournalist, she writes regularly for several major magazines and is the author of eleven cookbooks.

ARTHUR SCHWARTZ

Arthur Schwartz is the creator and editor of "Good Living," a weekly food and drink section in the New York *Daily News,* to which he also contributes a restaurant column. Although he travels widely in Europe and the United States in search of regional recipes, his particular interest is Italian food, and he is preparing a gastronomic guide to Italy.

ELIZABETH ALSTON

Born in England, Elizabeth Alston received her cooking training at the Cordon Bleu Cookery School in London, where she was awarded its Grande Diplôme. She has been the food editor of *Look, Family Health,* and *Redbook* magazines. She wrote *The Best of Natural Eating Around the World* and co-authored *The ABCs of Diabetic Cooking and Dining.* She is presently the food editor of *Woman's Day* magazine.

ROWENA HUBBARD

Rowena Hubbard, a home economist and nutritionist, has worked as a dietician and director of consumer affairs for several corporations and written hundreds of recipe leaflets and cookbooks, including *California Cooks.* Currently she is a managing partner of Anderson, Miller & Hubbard, food publicists in San Francisco.

Egg & Cheese Menus
GREAT MEALS FOR FOUR IN AN HOUR OR LESS

Convenient, economical, and above all versatile, eggs and cheese are prized by the world's great cuisines. Used alone or in combination, these foods are the basis for hundreds of highly nutritious dishes. Both eggs and cheese are good sources of vitamins, minerals, and protein. Eggs contain potassium, iron, calcium, and all the vitamins except C. Cheese has its own complete protein, casein, which contains every essential amino acid.

Eggs and cheese have been dietary staples for thousands of years. Prehistoric people undoubtedly ate wild birds' eggs, and fowl were domesticated in the Indus Valley around 2500 B.C. Although drawings of what appears to be cheese were found on stone tablets dated to 4000 B.C., a popular legend attributes its discovery to an early traveler who set off across the desert with a day's supply of milk in his pouch. Upon reaching his destination, he found that the milk had coagulated. Apparently rennet, an enzyme in the pouch (which was made from a sheep's stomach), when heated by the sun, caused the milk to separate into whey (a watery liquid) and curds (soft white lumps), resembling a crude cottage cheese.

From these beginnings, the production of eggs and cheese has grown to a big business. Despite the fact that both eggs and cheese are sources of cholesterol (which might be connected to heart disease), Americans consume an estimated 261 eggs and 21 pounds of cheese per person a year. The popularity of these two foods obviously stems from their diverse uses. Whether eggs are beaten, baked, poached, or boiled, and whether cheese is served sliced from the wheel or melted in an omelet, both provide endless inspiration for simple and elegant meals any time of day throughout the year.

On the following pages, nine of America's most talented cooks present 27 complete menus featuring egg- and cheese-based meals. Each menu can be prepared in an hour or less. The cooks use fresh produce and no powdered sauces, bottled dressings, or other dubious shortcuts. Additional ingredients (vinegars, spices, herbs, and so on) are all high quality yet widely available in supermarkets or, occasionally, in specialty food shops. Each menu serves four people.

The cooks and the test kitchen staff have planned the meals for appearance as well as taste, as the accompanying photographs show: The vegetables are brilliant and fresh, the visual combinations appetizing. The table settings feature bright colors, simple flower arrangements, and attractive, but not necessarily expensive, serving dishes.

For each menu, the Editors, with advice from the cooks, suggest wine and other beverages. And there are suggestions for the use of leftovers and for complementary desserts. On each menu page, too, you will find a range of other tips, from an easy way to make an egg *roulade* to advice for selecting the freshest produce. All recipes have been tested meticulously to ensure that even a relatively inexperienced cook can complete a menu within an hour.

BEFORE YOU START
Great Meals in Minutes is designed for efficiency and ease. This book will work best for you if you follow these suggestions:

1. Refresh your memory with the few simple cooking techniques on the following pages. They will quickly become second nature and will help you to produce professional-quality meals in minutes.

2. Read the menus before you shop. Each lists the ingredients you will need in the order that you would expect to shop for them in a supermarket. Many items will already be on your pantry shelf.

3. Check the equipment list on page 16. Good sharp knives and pots and pans of the right shape and material are essential for making great meals in minutes. This may be the time to buy a few things. The right equipment can turn cooking from a necessity into a creative experience.

4. Set out everything you need before you start to cook: The lists at the beginning of each menu tell just what is required.

5. Remove your meat, fish, and eggs from the refrigerator early enough for them to reach room temperature.

6. Follow the start-to-finish steps for each menu. This way, you can be sure of having the entire meal ready to serve in an hour.

SELECTING EGGS
Before you buy eggs, look for the United States Department of Agriculture (USDA) shield on the carton. It means that the eggs are federally inspected and classified. Some small egg packers, who follow equally rigid state inspection standards, will mark their egg cartons with a state shield rather than that of the USDA.

Whether used alone or in combination, eggs and cheese are the basis for hundreds of creative meals. Here are the ingredients for an herb and Cheddar soufflé—or perhaps an omelet.

Eggs are marketed by grade and size standards established by the USDA. Grade indicates the interior and exterior quality of the egg—the condition of the white and yolk, the size of the air pocket, and the cleanliness, smoothness, and shape of the shell. The grades in descending order of quality are AA, A, B, and C. Both AA and A eggs are excellent for cooking although some fastidious cooks prefer to use only AA eggs when appearance is important because they do not spread out when broken. The lower grades are just as nutritious, but are better for scrambling or baking since the yolks tend to break easily. Grade B and C eggs are usually sold to bakeries or the food industry and rarely appear in supermarkets.

Size is determined by minimum net weight per dozen. There are six egg-weight classes set by the USDA, ranging from jumbo (30 ounces per dozen) to peewee (15 ounces per dozen). Large eggs (24 ounces per dozen) are the most commonly sold and, unless otherwise stated, most recipes in this and other cookbooks call for them. If you are price conscious, a guideline to follow in buying eggs is that if there is more than a 7-cent difference between two sizes, the smaller size is the more economical.

When buying eggs, open the carton to make sure that all the eggs are there and that they are clean and uncracked. Damaged eggs may contain bacteria that can cause food poisoning. If any eggs crack before you get home, use them as soon as possible in a recipe that calls for thoroughly cooked eggs, such as a cake.

STORING EGGS

All fresh eggs require refrigeration. Eggs left out at room temperature will deteriorate more in one day than in one week of refrigeration. Never rinse eggs before storing them—you will wash away the light protective coating of tasteless mineral oil that is sprayed onto most eggs to seal their porous shells. Eggs stored large end up in their carton in the coldest part of the refrigerator should keep for five weeks. Do not store eggs near onions or other aromatic foods or the eggs may absorb the aromas through their shells. Hard-boiled eggs in their shells should be refrigerated as soon as possible after they cook and be used within a week. Shelled hard-boiled eggs placed in an airtight container or submerged in cold water will last two days in the refrigerator before becoming tough.

To determine if an unopened egg is raw or cooked, spin the egg on its point on a flat surface. If the egg is hard-boiled, it will spin like a top; if it is raw, it will fall over. Better yet, mark your hard-boiled eggs with an "X" to identify them.

If a recipe calls for egg whites only, you can store any unbroken yolks in water in a covered container to use within a day or two. If a recipe calls for only the yolks, the unused whites may be stored in a covered jar for up to ten days. Use extra yolks for preparing mayonnaise, custard, butter-cream frosting, hollandaise sauce and its variations, egg pastry, milk shakes, eggnogs, and Welsh rarebits. Yolks can also be used to glaze pastry and to make potato croquettes.

Use extra whites for meringue, mousse, for boiled cake frostings and fillings, fruit sherbets, angel food cake, and for clarifying stocks and coating fish fillets before breading. Whites make a good egg wash for pastries, too.

You can always add extra whites or yolks to scrambled eggs, or cook them separately and then sieve them to use as an attractive garnish for a soup or salad.

Freeze egg whites in an ice cube tray (one to a compartment) and then unmold them into a plastic bag when frozen, or freeze them in a plastic freezer container, sealed tightly and labeled with the date and the number of whites it contains. Two tablespoons of thawed whites equal one fresh white.

Egg yolks and whole eggs need to be treated prior to freezing, otherwise they will become gelatinous when thawed. Add ⅛ teaspoon salt or 1½ teaspoons sugar or corn syrup to 4 egg yolks or to 2 whole eggs and freeze them in a tightly sealed container labeled with the date and contents. Thaw as directed for whites (1 tablespoon of thawed yolk equals 1 large fresh yolk; 3 tablespoons of thawed whole egg equal 1 fresh whole egg).

Use thawed egg whites and yolks as soon as possible, in recipes that will be thoroughly cooked. *Do not* refreeze thawed whites or yolks.

TESTING FOR FRESHNESS

Egg freshness has no bearing on its nutritional value, but freshness does affect both how an egg cooks and, ultimately, how it tastes. Very fresh eggs are best for poaching and frying because they hold their shape better. On the other hand, very fresh eggs, when hard-boiled, do not peel easily. Older eggs are fine for boiling, scrambling, or baking, when appearance is not important.

Measuring an egg's buoyancy is said to be one test for freshness. Put the whole egg in a bowl of cold water. A newly laid egg, with only a tiny air pocket, is heavy and will sink to the bottom of the bowl. A week-old egg, with a large air pocket, is more buoyant and will tilt, large end up, in the water. A three-week-old egg, with an even larger air pocket, is even more buoyant and will stand upright in the water. An egg that is too old to eat will float to the surface.

HANDLING EGGS

Many cooks forget that for best results eggs need special handling. The following tips will improve your egg cookery:

Separating

Eggs separate more easily if they are thoroughly chilled. Set out two clean bowls, then separate the eggs one at a time. Crack the egg shell by sharply tapping the center of the shell on the edge of one of the bowls. With your fingers, carefully break the egg in half over one bowl, allowing some of the white to drop into the bowl, but catching the yolk in one of the shell halves. Gently pour the yolk back and forth between the shell halves, allowing the rest of the white to slide into the bowl. When the white is completely separated, drop the yolk into the other bowl. Be careful not to let any yolk fall into the bowl containing the whites. Use a moistened paper towel to remove any egg-shell

1. Crack egg against side of bowl.

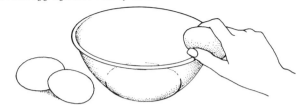

2. Separate egg by pouring back and forth between halves of shell until the entire white has dropped into one bowl.

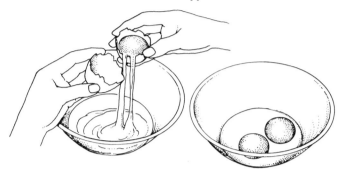

chips or traces of yolk from the whites. Some cooks prefer to use an egg separator, available at most supermarkets.

Beating
Although eggs separate better when chilled, they will produce greater volume if they are at room temperature when beaten. Let the eggs sit at room temperature for half an hour or put the whole eggs into a bowl of warm water for a few minutes before beating. If a recipe calls for slightly beaten whole eggs, use a fork or whisk to beat the eggs until the yolks and whites are just blended. For well-beaten whole eggs, use an electric mixer, egg beater, or whisk, and beat until the eggs are frothy and evenly colored. To beat yolks only, use an electric mixer at high speed or beat rapidly with a fork or whisk until the yolks thicken.

When beating whites, use either a large glass, china, stainless-steel, or copper bowl (do not use plastic) and be sure that the bowl and beaters are free of any grease or yolk, which will keep the whites from expanding properly. To beat whites with an electric mixer, begin at slow speed and beat until the whites produce small bubbles. Then turn the speed to high and beat until the whites are the required consistency. "Foamy" whites will be liquid and should flow easily. "Soft peak" whites are moist and shiny and form peaks that fold over when the beaters are removed. "Stiff peak" whites are still moist but form peaks that remain stiff when the beaters are removed.

For the stiffest whites, you can add ¼ teaspoon of cream of tartar for each two whites just after beating to the foamy stage; cream of tartar supplies the acidity that helps the whites to rise while keeping them stable. (Do not add cream of tartar if you are using a copper bowl, or it will turn the whites green.) The best way to make sure that egg whites are properly stiff is to perform the "tilt test." When you think the whites are stiff, stop beating and tilt the bowl; if the whites slide down the side of the bowl, resume beating them until they cling to the bowl. You

should be able to invert the bowl and have the beaten whites stay put. Overbeaten whites look dull and dry, will break apart when combined with other ingredients, and will collapse once they are heated. For the best results, beat the whites just before you need them so they do not deflate.

Incorporating
When adding whole eggs or egg yolks to a hot mixture, always add a small amount of the hot mixture to the eggs or yolks first to warm them (this is called "tempering," and it prevents the yolks from curdling), then gradually add the warmed eggs to the hot mixture, stirring constantly.

Folding beaten egg whites into another mixture should be done at the last moment. Use a rubber spatula to gently cut the whites into the mixture, moving from the top-center down to the bottom of the bowl and then up the sides. Turn the bowl slightly after each cut to ensure even dispersion.

TYPES OF CHEESE
Natural cheeses are made by coagulating milk, draining the liquid whey from the curds, and then collecting the curds. Subsequent pressing, curing, and flavoring processes produce the many varieties of cheese. Cheeses are grouped into four categories by texture and consistency: soft, semisoft, firm, and hard. Soft cheeses include the fresh (unripened) types, such as cottage cheese and cream cheese, as well as slightly ripened cheeses like Brie and Camembert. Semisoft cheeses include Muenster, Roquefort, and Gorgonzola. Firm cheeses have a lower moisture content than the soft and semisoft varieties. Cheddars and Swiss cheeses, such as Emmenthaler and Gruyère, are considered firm. Hard cheeses, which are aged until they are dry and granular, are ideal for grating and include Parmesan and Romano.

CHEESES IN THIS VOLUME
The cheeses listed below are recommended by the cooks for recipes in this volume. If a substitute is possible, it is indicated within the recipe.

Ricotta: This soft cheese, which originated in Italy, is made from whey and resembles cottage cheese. It is most often sold in plastic- or wax-coated cartons and is available in the dairy section of most supermarkets. Because it is runnier, cottage cheese is not a good substitute for ricotta. Elizabeth Alston uses ricotta in her broccoli *roulade* (page 90).

Gorgonzola: Blue-green veins run through the cream-colored interior of this whole-milk semisoft cheese, originally produced only in Italy but now made in the United States as well. Gorgonzola has a crumbly texture and a piquant flavor that sharpens with aging. Howard Helmer and Arlene Wanderman combine it with chicken in a quiche (page 49).

Smoked Gouda: A semisoft cheese made from whole or partly skimmed milk, smoked Gouda is flavored by natural smoking in much the same way meats are smoked. Elizabeth Alston's Ham and Smoked Cheese Bake (pages 86–87) includes smoked Gouda.

Gruyère: Made in France and Switzerland, this firm whole-milk cheese, prized for its melting quality, has a creamy yellow interior with small holes and a distinctive, nutty flavor. Ann Cashion's Carrot and Bacon Gratin (page 45) is topped with Gruyère.

Swiss: Swiss cheese is the popular name for whole-milk cheese with large irregularly shaped holes. When actually produced in Switzerland, this cheese is called Emmenthaler. It has a springy texture and a mild, nutty flavor and is used by Howard Helmer and Arlene Wanderman in their Reuben Omelets (page 54).

Parmesan: Made from partly skimmed milk, this straw-colored, piquant cheese has a hard, granular texture and is good for grating. For the best-tasting Parmesan (far superior to the pre-grated product), buy a fresh chunk from your supermarket or cheese shop and grate it as you need it. Arthur Schwartz sprinkles grated Parmesan over fried eggs (page 81).

Romano: Another hard cheese that originated in Italy, Romano is made from partly skimmed cow's or sheep's milk. Its taste is similar to, but sharper than, Parmesan. Douglas Oaks uses grated Romano as well as Gruyère in his Baked Eggs in Idaho Potatoes (page 21).

SHOPPING FOR CHEESE

Cheese shops are the best sources for cheese, although a supermarket or specialty food store with a high turnover is also a good place to buy cheese. In a cheese shop, the clerks will advise you about a particular cheese and its merits and offer samples. Retailers generally receive cheese in large wheels, blocks, or cylinders. Have your cheese cut to order so you get only as much as you need and can be confident of its quality and freshness.

STORING CHEESE

To remain fresh and unspoiled, cheese should be sealed in foil or plastic wrap, then stored in the refrigerator, preferably in a cheese container with a tight-fitting lid. Highly perishable soft cheese should be kept in its container and eaten within a week. Harder cheeses may keep for several months in the refrigerator, although their flavors will intensify. If you use only a small portion, rewrap the cut surface of the cheese so no air can reach it. If a cheese dries out in the refrigerator, it may be grated and stored in a tightly closed container.

Firm to hard cheese may be wrapped in plastic and frozen. Thaw the cheese in the refrigerator 24 to 48 hours before you need it. Some cheeses, such as Parmesan, can be grated frozen.

COOKING WITH EGGS AND CHEESE

The most important thing to remember when cooking with eggs and cheese is to use a low to medium temperature (except for omelets) and to monitor the cooking time. If you cook an egg at too high a heat, or for too long at a low heat, the whites will shrink and become tough and rubbery, and the yolks will toughen and may turn greenish-gray.

Too much heat or too-long cooking also harms cheese; it will turn stringy and rubbery as its fats are drawn out. You should add cheese to sauces or omelets at the last minute and bake cheese-based dishes in a moderate oven.

If you cook an egg whole, the white firms more quickly than the yolk. If you blend the white and yolk, they set at the same rate. If you stir the egg constantly while cooking, as you do for scrambled eggs, the egg remains soft and moist. Left unstirred, the egg thickens and becomes a cohesive whole, as in an omelet.

The basic techniques described below will help you prepare the recipes in this volume. Many of the recipes call for eggs alone, some for a combination of eggs and cheese.

Whole Egg Cookery

Frying: When you fry eggs, cook them in a skillet in a small amount of hot fat. The fat should be hot enough to sizzle when a drop of water is added; do not let it brown. When the fat is ready, break the eggs into the skillet and reduce the heat immediately to prevent the whites from becoming rubbery. For "sunny-side-up" eggs, baste the yolks by spooning hot fat over them until the tops set. Alternatively, set the yolks by putting a lid on the skillet to trap and reflect the heat. To prepare "over-easy" eggs, flip the eggs with a spatula when the whites are firm, then turn off the heat; when the white surrounding the yolks has set, remove the eggs from the skillet. Arthur Schwartz serves fried eggs with asparagus (page 81).

Poaching: When you poach eggs, you cook them in liquid that has been heated to boiling and then reduced to a simmer; this keeps the whites from becoming rubbery. It is easiest to poach eggs one at a time. Crack each egg into a small cup, then stir the simmering water to make a small whirlpool. Slide the egg into the whirlpool (the motion of the water will keep the white from spreading) and simmer 3 to 5 minutes. Remove it with a slotted spoon and drain on a paper or dish towel. If you wish, you can neaten the eggs by trimming the whites. If you do not plan to use the cooked eggs right away, immediately put them into a dish of ice water to stop the cooking process and to keep them moist. Poached eggs can be refrigerated this way for up to 24 hours. To reheat, dip them briefly in hot water. You can use broth, milk, water, or some other liquid to poach eggs.

Hard boiling: Eggs that are at least a week old are preferable for hard boiling since they can be peeled more easily. To prevent eggs from cracking and leaking during cooking, pierce each with a straight pin at the large end, penetrating the membrane. Put the pierced eggs into a pot of cold water to cover, bring the water just to a boil, then lower the temperature to a simmer. After 8 to 10 minutes the yolk and white of a large egg will be firmly set. If you cook an egg too long, or leave it at a boil, the white becomes rubbery, the yolk dries out, and a thin green layer forms between the surface of the yolk and the white.

When the hard-boiled eggs are ready, drain the hot water and add cold water to the pan to stop the cooking and to cool the eggs for easy handling. To peel a hard-boiled egg, gently crack it all over by tapping it or rolling it on a tabletop. Then roll the egg between your hands to loosen the shell, and peel it under running water starting at the large end. Hard-boiled eggs can be served whole, sliced, or crumbled or grated for a garnish. Copeland Marks offers halved hard-boiled eggs topped with stir-fried red pepper (page 31).

Baking: Baked eggs are cooked in an ovenproof dish or perhaps in an edible container such as a potato shell, which Douglas Oaks uses (page 21). The surface of the egg is usually covered with a sauce or other liquid to keep it moist. Penelope Casas (pages 58–59) bakes egg yolks in hollowed-out rolls and covers the yolks with a crown of stiffly beaten egg whites to protect them.

Beaten Egg Cookery

Scrambling: To prepare scrambled eggs, first beat the yolks and whites together. For uniformly yellow scrambled eggs, beat the eggs thoroughly; for a marbled effect, beat the eggs until the yolks just streak the whites. Pour the beaten eggs into a skillet containing hot fat and over low heat stir them constantly to produce creamy, moist curds. Remove the pan from the heat while the eggs are slightly undercooked because they will continue to cook for a few moments. Jean Anderson scrambles eggs with salt cod, onions, and green olives (pages 68–69).

For soft-set scrambled eggs, which have a velvety custard-like consistency, cook the beaten eggs in the generously buttered top section of a double boiler over sim-

mering water and stir constantly. The heat of the water will cook the eggs slowly and gently. For a skillet "double boiler," follow Penelope Casas's directions (page 65).

Omelet making: Cooking a successful omelet takes less than a minute. Be sure to bring the eggs to room temperature before using them. To keep the beaten eggs from sticking to the pan, a nonstick or well-seasoned omelet pan is essential (see the box, Seasoning an Omelet Pan, on page 12). Omelets should be cooked over high heat so that the bottom firms quickly and the top remains creamy; if an omelet cooks too slowly it dries out and toughens. Have the pan and the butter hot before you pour in the lightly beaten eggs, then stir a few times with the flat of a fork. As the underside of the omelet begins to set, lift the edges and tilt the pan to allow the uncooked egg to run to the bottom. While the top of the omelet is still moist, you can add a filling of your choice, then fold or roll the omelet and slide it onto a plate. Howard Helmer and Arlene Wanderman have a slightly different omelet-making technique for their Reuben Omelets (page 54), and Copeland Marks also has his own technique for the Shrimp, Tofu, and Tomato Omelets (pages 32–33).

An omelet can take different forms. For instance, a puffy (or soufflé) omelet, such as Ann Cashion prepares (page 44), is achieved by beating the whites and yolks separately and folding them together just before cooking. The key is to combine them gently, so that you maintain as much volume as possible. As with the basic omelet, a well-seasoned pan is important.

A *frittata* is an open-faced Italian omelet. Unlike the classic French omelet, a *frittata* contains more added ingredients (such as shredded vegetables) than eggs and is not folded but served flat. Cook a *frittata* slowly over moderate heat until the eggs are set but not dried out. When the underside is relatively firm, flip the *frittata* over with a spatula or invert it onto a plate and slide it back into the pan. Rowena Hubbard offers a variation on a *frittata* (page 102), in which she firms the eggs by baking them in the oven rather than on top of the stove. Elizabeth Alston's avocado and fresh coriander *frittata* (page 92) is not flipped at all but allowed to cook through until almost firm.

Soufflé making: Soufflés are light, puffy creations that are impressive at any meal. A true soufflé is made from a thick white sauce blended with beaten egg yolks and leavened with stiffly beaten egg whites. Although the idea of preparing a soufflé intimidates many cooks, mastering the technique is simple. Separate the eggs immediately after removing them from the refrigerator and let them come to room temperature while you continue the preparation. Next prepare the soufflé dish or straight-sided casserole: Generously butter the dish, then dust with flour, grated cheese, or sugar (for a sweet soufflé). If you suspect that your soufflé may rise well over the rim of the dish (as it bakes, a soufflé often doubles or triples in volume), you should make a soufflé collar for the dish (see pages 51–52); be sure to butter the collar.

Beat the egg whites until they stand in stiff peaks. Then fold the whites immediately into the soufflé base. Do not overmix or the whites will deflate; a few streaks of un-mixed egg white are acceptable. Pour the soufflé into the prepared dish and bake as directed. *Do not* open the oven door to peek during the first 20 minutes of baking or your soufflé may collapse. Soufflés do not hold successfully, so it is better to have your guests waiting for the soufflé than the soufflé waiting for your guests. Howard Helmer and Arlene Wanderman present a Spinach and Smoked Salmon Soufflé (pages 51–52).

GENERAL COOKING TECHNIQUES
Sautéing
Sautéing is a form of quick frying, with no cover on the pan. In French, *sauter* means "to jump," which is what vegetables or small pieces of food do when you shake the sauté pan. The purpose is to brown the food lightly and seal in the juices, sometimes before further cooking. This technique has three critical elements: the right pan, the proper temperature, and dry food.

The sauté pan: A proper sauté pan is 10 to 12 inches in diameter and has 2- to 3-inch straight sides; it allows you to turn the food pieces and still keep the fat from spattering. It has a heavy bottom that can be moved back and forth easily across a burner.

The best material (and the most expensive) for a sauté pan is tin-lined copper because it is a superior heat conductor. Heavy-gauge cast aluminum works well but will discolor acidic food like tomatoes. Another option is to select a heavy-duty sauté pan made of strong, heat-conducting aluminum alloys. This type of professional cookware is smooth and stick-resistant. Be sure you buy a sauté pan with a handle that is long and comfortable to hold, and with a tight-fitting cover, since many recipes call for covered cooking following the initial sautéing.

Use a sauté pan large enough to hold the pieces of food without crowding, or sauté in two batches. The heat of the fat and the air spaces around and between the pieces facilitate browning. Crowding results in steaming, which releases juices.

Keep the pieces of food moving in the pan using a wooden spatula or tongs as you shake the pan over the burner. If the food sticks, as it occasionally will, a metal spatula will loosen it best. Turn the food pieces so that all surfaces come into contact with the hot fat. Do not use a fork when sautéing meat; piercing the meat will allow the juices to escape.

The fat: Half butter and half vegetable oil is perfect for most sautéing: It heats to high temperatures without burning, yet allows a rich butter flavor. For cooking, un-salted butter tastes best and adds no extra salt.

If you prefer an all-butter flavor, clarify the butter before you begin. This means removing the milk solids (which scorch easily) from the oils. To clarify butter, heat it in a small heavy saucepan over medium heat and, using a cooking spoon, skim off the foam as it rises to the top and discard it. Keep skimming until no more foam appears. Pour off the remaining liquid, which is the clarified butter, leaving the milky residue at the bottom of the pan. Clarify butter as you need it, or to save time make a large quantity and store it in your refrigerator for up to three weeks.

Some sautéing recipes in this book call for olive oil, which imparts a delicious and distinctive flavor of its own and is less sensitive than butter to high heat. Never-theless, even the finest olive oil has some residue of fruit pulp, which will occasionally scorch. Watch carefully when you sauté in olive oil; discard any scorched oil and start with fresh, if necessary.

To sauté properly, heat the fat until it is hot but not smoking. When you see small bubbles on top of the fat, lower the heat because it is on the verge of smoking. When using butter and oil together, add butter to the hot oil. After the foam from the melting butter subsides, you are ready to sauté. If the temperature of the fat is just right, the food will sizzle when you put it in the pan.

Seasoning an Omelet Pan

To produce perfect omelets, you need a well-seasoned or nonstick heavy-bottomed pan with sloping sides. Omelet pans range from 7 to 12 inches. You may choose an alumi-num, steel, or cast-iron pan, but before using it you must clean and season it well unless it is nonstick. The "season-ing" is a coat of oil, which adheres permanently to the interior surface to prevent food from sticking. Ideally, the pan should be used only for omelets and not for cooking other foods. To season the pan, first wash it in hot water, scouring the inside surface with fine steel wool and soap. Rinse and dry the pan thoroughly.

If your pan has an ovenproof handle, pour in a table-spoon of cooking oil and spread it around with a pastry brush or paper towel to coat the interior, then heat the pan in a 375-degree oven for about half an hour. Cool it, then wipe it out with a paper towel. The pan is now seasoned.

If your pan does not have an ovenproof handle, put 1 inch of oil into the pan and heat it on the stove until the oil is very hot but not smoking (about 375 degrees). Carefully remove the pan from the heat and let it cool, then pour off the oil (if the oil has not been heated to the smoking point, it can be reused for cooking). Wipe out the pan.

Before using either type of omelet pan, sprinkle it with a little coarse salt, rub it with an oily paper towel, and wipe it out. To clean the pan after cooking an omelet, rub the pan with salt and a damp paper towel to remove any food residue. If you find it necessary to wash the pan, you may need to reseason it; avoid scouring or using harsh de-tergents. Always rub the interior of the pan with a few drops of oil before you put it away.

Making Chicken Stock

Although canned chicken broth or stock is all right for emergencies, homemade chicken stock has a rich flavor that is hard to match. Moreover, the commercial broths—particularly the canned ones—are likely to be oversalted.

To make your own stock, save chicken parts as they accumulate and put them in a bag in the freezer; then have a rainy-day stock-making session, using one of the recipes here. The skin from a yellow onion will add color; the optional veal bone will add extra flavor and richness to the stock.

Basic Chicken Stock

3 pounds bony chicken parts, such as wings, back, and neck
1 veal knuckle (optional)
3 quarts cold water
1 yellow unpeeled onion, stuck with 2 cloves
2 stalks celery with leaves, cut in two
12 crushed peppercorns
2 carrots, scraped and cut into 2-inch lengths
4 sprigs parsley
1 bay leaf
1 tablespoon fresh thyme, or 1 teaspoon dried
Salt (optional)

1. Wash chicken parts and veal knuckle (if you are using it) and drain. Place in large soup kettle or stockpot (any big pot) with the remaining ingredients—except salt. Cover pot and bring to a boil over medium heat.

2. Lower heat and simmer stock, partly covered, 2 to 3 hours. Skim foam and scum from top of stock several times. Add salt to taste after stock has cooked 1 hour.

3. Strain stock through fine sieve placed over large bowl. Discard chicken pieces, vegetables, and seasonings. Let stock cool uncovered (this will speed cooling process). When completely cool, refrigerate. Fat will rise and congeal conveniently at top. You may skim it off and discard it or leave it as protective covering for stock.

Yield: About 10 cups.

The flavor of chicken stock comes from the bones (as well as the seasonings and vegetables) rather than the meat. The longer you cook the bones, the better the stock. If you would like to poach a whole chicken and want to make a good, strong stock at the same time, this highly economical recipe will accomplish both aims at once.

Strong Chicken Stock

10 cups homemade chicken stock (yield of recipe at left)
1 bay leaf
1 stalk celery
1 carrot, scraped
1 yellow onion, unpeeled
1 whole broiler or fryer (about 3 pounds)

1. Add stock, bay leaf, and vegetables to kettle large enough to hold them and chicken. Bring to a boil over medium heat.

2. Add chicken, breast up, and allow liquid to return to a simmer. Reduce heat and poach chicken with lid slightly ajar.

3. After 40 minutes, test for doneness. Insert long-handled spoon into chicken cavity and remove chicken to platter.

4. When chicken is cool enough to handle, but still warm, debone it, reserving meat for salads or sandwiches but returning skin and bones to cooking pot. Continue to simmer, uncovered, until stock has reduced by half. Proceed as in step 3 of basic stock recipe, left.

Added Touch: If you have time and want a particularly rich-looking stock, put the chicken bones in a shallow baking pan and brown them under the broiler for 10 minutes before you add them to the stock.

Stock freezes well and will keep for three months in the freezer. Use small containers for convenience and freeze in pre-measured amounts: a cup, or half a cup. Or pour the cooled stock into ice cube trays, then remove the frozen cubes and store in a plastic bag. You can drop these frozen cubes directly into your saucepan.

Steaming
Steaming is a fast and nutritious way to cook vegetables and other food. Bring water to a boil in a steamer. Place food in the steaming basket or rack over the liquid and cover the pan, periodically checking the water level. Keeping the food above the liquid preserves vitamins and minerals while cooking.

Stir Frying
This is the basic cooking method for Chinese cuisine. This fast-cook technique requires very little oil, and the foods—which you stir continuously—fry quickly over a very high heat. Stir frying is ideal for cooking bite-size, shredded, or thinly sliced portions of vegetables, fish, meat, or poultry alone or in combination. Copeland Marks uses this cooking method for his Indonesian Fried Rice (page 31).

Baking
Baking is dry-heat cooking (usually in an oven) of foods such as casseroles, poultry parts, small cuts of meat, fish, vegetables, and, of course, breads and pastries. Some foods are baked tightly covered to retain their juices and flavors; others, such as breads, cakes, and cookies, are baked in open pans to release moisture.

Poaching
You poach meat, fish, chicken, fruit, and eggs in very hot liquid in a pan on top of the stove (see page 11 for egg poaching instructions). You can use water, or better still, beef, chicken, or fish stock, or a combination of stock and white wine, or even cream as the poaching liquid.

Glazing
Glazing vegetables in their cooking liquid, butter, and a little sugar or honey gives them a slight sheen as the butter and sugar reduce to a syrupy consistency. Glazing enhances the flavor and appearance of vegetables, and they need no additional sauce. Douglas Oaks glazes Brussels sprouts (page 21).

Pantry (for this volume)

A well-stocked, properly organized pantry is essential for preparing great meals in the shortest time possible. Whether your pantry consists of a small refrigerator and two or three shelves over the sink, or a large freezer, refrigerator, and entire room just off the kitchen, you must protect staples from heat and light.

In maintaining your pantry, follow these rules:

1. Store staples by kind and date. Canned goods, canisters, and spices need a separate shelf, or a separate spot on a shelf. Date all staples—shelved, refrigerated, or frozen—by writing the date directly on the package or on a bit of masking tape. Then put the oldest ones in front to be sure you use them first.

2. Store flour, sugar, and other dry ingredients in canisters or jars with tight lids. Glass and clear plastic allow you to see at a glance how much remains.

3. Keep a running grocery list so that you can note when a staple is half gone, and be sure to stock up.

ON THE SHELF:

Anchovies
Anchovy fillets, both flat and rolled, come oil-packed, in tins. If you buy whole, salt-packed anchovies, they must be cleaned under running water, skinned, and boned. To bone, separate the fish with your fingers and slip out the backbone.

Capers
Capers are usually packed in vinegar and less frequently in salt. If you use the latter, you should rinse them under cold water before using them.

Cornstarch
Less likely to lump than flour, cornstarch is an excellent thickener for sauces. Substitute in the following proportions: 1 tablespoon cornstarch to 2 of flour.

Cream of tartar

Dried fruits
golden raisins

Dried mushrooms
Imported from Asia and Europe, dried mushrooms provide rich flavor to cooked dishes. Stored airtight in a cool place they will keep up to a year.

Flour
all-purpose, bleached or unbleached

Garlic
Store in a cool, dry, well-ventilated place. Garlic powder and garlic salt are not adequate substitutes for fresh garlic.

Herbs and spices
The flavor of fresh herbs is much better than that of dried. Fresh herbs should be refrigerated and used as soon as possible. The following herbs are perfectly acceptable dried, but buy in small amounts, store airtight in dry area away from heat and light, and use as quickly as possible. In measuring herbs, remember that one part dried will equal three parts fresh. *Note:* Dried chives and parsley should not be on your shelf, since they have little or no flavor; frozen chives are acceptable. Buy whole spices rather than ground, as they keep their flavor much longer. Grind spices at home and store as directed for herbs.

allspice
basil
bay leaves
caraway seeds
cardamom, whole or
    ground
Cayenne pepper
cinnamon
cloves, whole and ground
coriander, whole and
    ground
cumin
curry powder
dill
fennel seeds
mustard (powdered)
nutmeg, whole and ground
oregano
paprika
pepper
    black peppercorns
    These are unripe pepper-
corns dried in their husks. Grind with a pepper mill for each use.
    white peppercorns
    These are the same as the black variety, but are picked ripe and husked. Use them in pale sauces when black pepper specks would spoil the appearance.
red pepper flakes (also
    called crushed red
    pepper)
rosemary
saffron
    Made from the dried stigmas of a species of crocus, this spice—the most costly of all seasonings—adds both color and flavor. Use sparingly.
salt
    Use coarse salt—commonly available as Kosher or sea—for its superior flavor, texture, and purity. Kosher salt and sea salt are less salty than table salt. Substitute in the following proportions: three-quarters teaspoon table salt equals just under one teaspoon Kosher or sea salt.
sesame seeds
tarragon
thyme
turmeric

Honey

Hot pepper sauce

Nuts, whole, chopped, or
    slivered
almonds
pecans
pine nuts (pignoli)
walnuts

Oils
corn, safflower, peanut,
    or vegetable
    Because these neutral-tasting oils have high smoking points, they are good for high-heat sautéing.
olive oil
    Olive oil ranges in color from pale yellow to dark green and in taste from mild and delicate to rich and fruity. Different olive oils can be used for different purposes: for example, lighter ones for cooking, stronger ones for salads. The finest quality olive oil is labeled extra-virgin or virgin.
sesame oil
    Dark amber-colored Oriental-style oil, used for seasoning; do not substitute light cold-pressed sesame oil.
walnut oil
    Rich and nutty tasting. It turns rancid easily, so keep it in a tightly closed container in the refrigerator.

Onions
Store all dry-skinned onions in a cool, dry, well-ventilated place.
red or Italian onions
    Zesty tasting and generally eaten raw. The perfect salad onion.
shallots
    The most subtle member of the onion family, the shallot has a delicate garlic flavor.
Spanish onions
    Very large with a sweet flavor, they are best for

stuffing and baking and are also eaten raw. Perfect for sandwiches.

yellow onions
All-purpose cooking onions, strong in taste.

Potatoes, boiling and baking
"New" potatoes are not a particular kind of potato, but any potato that has not been stored.

Rice
long-grain white rice
Slender grains, much longer than they are wide, that become light and fluffy when cooked and are best for general use.

Soy Sauce
Chinese
Usually quite salty and richly flavored—for cooking.

Japanese
Less salty and more delicate than Chinese—for use as a table sauce and in cooking.

Stock, chicken and beef
For maximum flavor and quality, your own stock is best (see recipe page 13), but canned stock, or broth, is adequate for most recipes and convenient to have on hand.

Sugar
light brown sugar
granulated sugar

Tomatoes
Italian plum tomatoes
Canned plum tomatoes (preferably imported) are an acceptable substitute for fresh.

Vinegars
apple cider vinegar (also called cider vinegar)
Use for a mild, fruity flavor.

balsamic vinegar
Aged vinegar with a complex sweet and sour taste

red and white wine vinegars

tarragon vinegar
A white wine vinegar flavored with fresh tarragon, it is especially good in salads.

Wines and spirits
sherry, dry
red wine, dry
white wine, dry

IN THE REFRIGERATOR:

Basil
Though fresh basil is widely available only in summer, try to use it whenever possible to replace dried; the flavor is markedly superior. Stand the stems, preferably with roots intact, in a jar of water, and loosely cover leaves with a plastic bag.

Bread crumbs
You need never buy bread crumbs. To make fresh crumbs, use fresh or day-old bread and process in food processor or blender. For dried, toast bread 30 minutes in preheated 250-degree oven, turning occasionally to prevent slices from browning. Proceed as for fresh. Store bread crumbs in an airtight container: fresh crumbs in the refrigerator, and dried crumbs in a cool, dry place. Either type may also be frozen for several weeks if tightly wrapped in a plastic bag.

Butter
Many cooks prefer unsalted butter because of its finer flavor and because it does not burn as easily as salted.

Cheese
Cheddar cheese, sharp
A firm cheese, ranging in color from nearly white to yellow. Cheddar is a versatile cooking cheese.

Gorgonzola
Semisoft whole-milk cheese with blue-green veining. A fine dessert cheese with fruit.

Gruyère
This firm cheese resembles Swiss, but has smaller holes and a sharper flavor. A quality Gruyère will have a slight "gleam" in its eyes, or holes.

Parmesan cheese
Avoid the pre-grated packaged variety; it is very expensive and almost flavorless. Buy Parmesan by the quarter- or half-pound wedge and grate as needed: 4 ounces produces about one cup of grated cheese. Romano, far less costly, can be substituted, but its flavor is considerably sharper—or try mixing the two.

Ricotta
Made from whey with whole or skim milk added, ricotta resembles cottage cheese but does not separate when cooked.

Romano
This Italian grating cheese may be made from sheep's milk (pecorino Romano) or cow's milk.

Smoked cheese
Gouda, Cheddar, Provolone, and mozzarella are among cheeses sometimes sold smoked. Try to find a naturally smoked product.

Swiss
Its sweet, nutlike flavor has made this a popular cheese and it is now made in many countries. The authentic Swiss product has the word "Switzerland" printed on the rind.

Chives
Refrigerate fresh chives wrapped in plastic. You may also buy small pots of growing chives—keep them on a windowsill and snip as needed.

Coriander
Also called *cilantro* or Chinese parsley, its pungent leaves resemble flat-leaf parsley. Keep in a glass of water covered with a plastic bag.

Cream
half-and-half
heavy cream
light cream
sour cream

Eggs
Will keep 4 to 5 weeks in refrigerator. For best results, bring to room temperature before using, except when separating.

Ginger, fresh
Found in the produce section. Wrap in a paper towel, then in plastic, and refrigerate; it will keep for about 1 month, but should be checked weekly for mold. To preserve it longer, place the whole ginger root in a small sherry-filled jar; it will last almost indefinitely, although not without changes in the ginger. Or, if you prefer, store it in the freezer, where it will last about 3 months. Newly purchased ginger need not be peeled.

Lemons
In addition to its many uses in cooking, a slice of lemon rubbed over cut apples and pears will keep them from discoloring. Do not substitute bottled juice or lemon extract.

Milk

Mint
Fresh mint will keep for a week if wrapped in a damp paper towel and enclosed in a plastic bag.

Mustards
The recipes in this book usually call for Dijon or coarse-ground mustard.

Parsley
The two most commonly available kinds of parsley are flat-leaf and curly; they can be used interchangeably when necessary. Flat-leaf parsley has a more distinctive flavor and is generally preferred in cooking. Curly parsley wilts less easily and is excellent for garnishing. Store parsley in a glass of water and cover loosely with a plastic bag. It will keep for a week in the refrigerator. Or wash and dry it, and refrigerate in a small plastic bag with a dry paper towel inside to absorb any moisture.

Scallions
Scallions have a mild onion flavor. Store wrapped in plastic.

Equipment

Proper cooking equipment makes the work light and is a good cook's most prized possession. You can cook expertly without a store-bought steamer or even a food processor, but basic pans, knives, and a few other items are indispensable. Below are the things you need—and some attractive options—for preparing the menus in this volume.

Pots and pans
Large kettle or stockpot
3 skillets (large, medium, small) with covers
Large skillet with ovenproof handle
2 heavy-gauge sauté pans, 10 to 12 inches in diameter, with covers and ovenproof handles
3 saucepans with covers (1-, 2-, and 4-quart capacities)
  Choose heavy-gauge enameled cast-iron, plain cast-iron, aluminum-clad stainless steel, and aluminum (but you need at least one saucepan that is not aluminum). Best—but very expensive—is tin-lined copper.
8-inch nonstick or well-seasoned omelet pan
Roasting pan
3 shallow baking pans (13 x 9 x 2-inch, 9 x 7-inch, and 8 x 8-inch)
2 cookie sheets (11 x 17-inch and 15 x 10-inch)
Medium-size soufflé dish
Large flameproof glass baking dish
Large ovenproof serving bowl
Heatproof serving platters
Four 8- to 12-ounce ramekins or individual soufflé dishes
10-inch quiche pan with removable bottom
Salad bowl

Knives
A carbon-steel knife takes a sharp edge but tends to rust. You must wash and dry it after each use; otherwise it can blacken foods and counter tops. Good-quality stainless steel knives, frequently honed, are less trouble and will serve just as well in the home kitchen. Never put a fine knife in the dishwasher. Rinse it, dry it, and put it away—but not loose in a drawer. Knives will stay sharp if they have their own storage rack.
Small paring knife
10-inch chef's knife
Bread knife (serrated edge)
Sharpening steel

Other cooking tools
2 sets of mixing bowls in graduated sizes, one set preferably glass or stainless steel
Colander, with a round base (stainless steel, aluminum, or enamel)
2 strainers in fine and coarse mesh
2 sets of measuring cups and spoons in graduated sizes
  One for dry ingredients, another for shortenings and liquids.
Cooking spoon
Slotted spoon
Long-handled wooden spoons
Wooden spatula (for stirring hot ingredients)
2 metal spatulas, or turners (for lifting hot foods from pans)
Slotted spatula
Nylon or nylon-coated spatula (for use with nonstick pans)
Rubber or vinyl spatula (for folding in ingredients)
Rolling pin
Grater (metal, with several sizes of holes)
  A rotary grater is handy for hard cheese.
Small wire whisk
Balloon whisk
Pair of metal tongs
Wooden board
Garlic press
Vegetable peeler
Mortar and pestle
Vegetable steamer
Ladle
Pastry brush for basting (a small, new paintbrush that is not nylon serves well)
Vegetable brush
Cooling rack
Kitchen shears
Kitchen timer
Aluminum foil
Paper towels
Plastic wrap
Waxed paper

Thin rubber gloves
Oven mitts or potholders

Electric appliances
Food processor or blender
  A blender will do most of the work required in this volume, but a food processor will do it more quickly and in larger volume. A food processor should be considered a necessity, not a luxury, for anyone who enjoys cooking.
Electric mixer

Optional cooking tools
Salad spinner
Egg separator
Egg slicer
Apple corer
Salad servers
Citrus juicer
  Inexpensive glass kind from the dime store will do.
Nutmeg grater
Zester
Roll of masking tape or white paper tape for labeling and dating

COLANDER

STRAINER

FOOD
PROCESSOR

RUBBER
SPATULA

MIXING BOWLS

SLOTTED
SPATULA

METAL
SPATULA

EGG SEPARATOR

SHARPENING STEEL

CHEF'S KNIFE

WHISK

GRATER

PARING KNIFE

SOUFFLÉ
DISH

SAUCEPANS

SAUTÉ PAN

Douglas Oaks

MENU 1 (Right)
Baked Eggs in Idaho Potatoes
Honey-Glazed Brussels Sprouts with Walnuts
Tomatoes Vinaigrette

MENU 2
Salmon Turbans with Béarnaise Sauce
Wild Rice with Pecans
Buttered Asparagus Spears

MENU 3
California Omelets
Snow Peas and Carrots Polonaise

When cooking for friends or for his own pleasure, Douglas Oaks loves nothing more than to open the refrigerator and prepare a meal with what is on hand. For him the challenge is in being innovative on the spot. Although his meals can be unorthodox, he usually achieves what he sets out to do: create a unified menu from disparate elements. The menus here, although carefully planned, reflect his spontaneity in the kitchen.

In Menu 1, he cooks the eggs in prebaked potato shells, rather than in traditional ramekins. The eggs are enhanced with three types of cheese and prosciutto. To accompany the main course, he offers honey-glazed Brussels sprouts and a salad of sliced tomatoes in a vinaigrette dressing.

Menu 2 is an elegant spring dinner. The salmon fillets are molded into individual turbans, each filled with baked egg and a mixture of mushrooms and green pepper. As a finishing touch, the cook tops the turbans with Béarnaise sauce (made from egg yolk, butter, and a wine and vinegar reduction seasoned with tarragon). Although Béarnaise is generally served with red meat, it also goes extremely well with eggs. Menu 3 features a large omelet filled with an unexpected combination of red peppers, chicken, hearts of palm, and cheese. Eggs reappear in the topping for the snow pea and carrot side dish.

For a hearty brunch, serve potato shells filled with prosciutto, eggs, and cheese—topped with sautéed vegetables. Color-complement the main dish with glazed Brussels sprouts and a tomato salad flavored with basil, fennel, and capers.

Baked Eggs in Idaho Potatoes
Honey-Glazed Brussels Sprouts with Walnuts
Tomatoes Vinaigrette

Brussels sprouts resemble miniature cabbages but are more delicately flavored. Buy Brussels sprouts that are compact, firm, and have a bright green color. Refrigerated unwashed in a plastic bag, they will keep for several days, but for best results use them quickly.

A very fresh egg white whipped into the salad dressing acts as a frothy suspension for the herbs and spices and helps to blend the ingredients for a fuller flavor. Crush the fennel seeds to release their oils before adding them to the dressing.

WHAT TO DRINK

A full-bodied dry white wine or a light-bodied dry red would go well with these baked eggs. Try a California Chardonnay or French Mâcon for white; a California Merlot, French Saint-Émilion, or Italian Chianti for red.

SHOPPING LIST AND STAPLES

8 slices prosciutto (about ¼ pound total weight)
4 large Idaho potatoes (about ¾ pound each)
1 pound fresh Brussels sprouts, or 10-ounce package frozen
2 medium-size tomatoes (about 1 pound total weight)
Medium-size red bell pepper
Medium-size green bell pepper
Small head Bibb or leaf lettuce
2 ounces mushrooms
Small bunch scallions
Small bunch watercress (optional)
Small bunch dill
Small bunch basil
9 small eggs
1 stick unsalted butter
2 ounces Gruyère cheese
2 ounces Romano cheese
2 ounces Swiss cheese
½ cup olive oil
2 tablespoons vegetable oil
2 tablespoons red wine vinegar
¼ cup honey
1¼ teaspoons capers
4-ounce package walnut pieces
1 teaspoon caraway seeds (optional)
½ teaspoon fennel seeds
Salt and freshly ground white pepper

UTENSILS

2 medium-size skillets
Vegetable steamer
Baking sheet
Shallow glass baking dish
Medium-size bowl, preferably stainless steel
Salad spinner (optional)
Measuring cups and spoons
Chef's knife
Paring knife
Wooden spoon
Mortar and pestle
Grater
Whisk
Vegetable scrub brush
Pastry brush

START-TO-FINISH STEPS

One hour ahead: If using frozen Brussels sprouts, set out to thaw.

1. Follow eggs recipe steps 1 and 2.
2. While potatoes are baking, follow tomatoes recipe steps 1 through 4 and eggs recipe steps 3 through 5.
3. When potatoes are done, follow eggs recipe steps 6 through 8.
4. While eggs are baking in potato shells, follow Brussels sprouts recipe steps 1 and 2.
5. Follow eggs recipe step 9.
6. Follow tomatoes recipe step 5 and Brussels sprouts recipe steps 3 and 4.
7. Follow eggs recipe step 10, and serve with Brussels sprouts and tomatoes.

RECIPES

Baked Eggs in Idaho Potatoes

4 large Idaho potatoes (about ¾ pound each)
2 tablespoons vegetable oil
2 ounces Gruyère cheese
2 ounces Romano cheese
2 ounces Swiss cheese
1 teaspoon caraway seeds (optional)
Small bunch scallions
Medium-size red bell pepper
2 ounces mushrooms

4 tablespoons unsalted butter
8 slices prosciutto (about ¼ pound total weight)
8 small eggs

1. Preheat oven to 400 degrees.
2. Scrub potatoes and dry thoroughly with paper towels. Liberally brush each potato with vegetable oil and lay on baking sheet. Bake 35 to 40 minutes, or until potato yields to pressure, but is still firm.
3. Grate cheeses to measure about ½ cup each; toss together. Toss cheeses with caraway seeds, if desired, and set mixture aside.
4. Trim scallions; wash, dry, and slice thinly to measure about ½ cup. Wash red pepper; halve, seed, remove membranes, and dice to measure about ½ cup. Wipe mushrooms with damp paper towels and dice finely to measure about ⅔ cup.
5. Heat 4 tablespoons unsalted butter in skillet. Add scallions, pepper, and mushrooms and sauté over medium heat about 3 minutes, until scallions are translucent.
6. Halve cooked potatoes lengthwise. Scoop out flesh, leaving ¼-inch-thick shell. Reserve flesh for another use. Place shells on baking sheet.
7. Sprinkle 1 to 1½ teaspoons grated cheese mixture into each potato and line shell with 1 slice of prosciutto, folding to fit, if necessary. Then break 1 egg into each shell.
8. Bake 8 to 10 minutes, or until eggs are barely set.
9. Remove potatoes from oven and turn oven to broil. Sprinkle with remaining cheese and top with sautéed vegetable mixture. Set aside until ready to serve.
10. Just before serving, broil 1 minute, or just until cheese has melted. Transfer 2 potato halves to each of 4 dinner plates and serve.

Honey-Glazed Brussels Sprouts with Walnuts

Small bunch dill
1 pound fresh Brussels sprouts, or 10-ounce package frozen, thawed
4 tablespoons unsalted butter
⅓ cup walnut pieces
¼ cup honey

1. Wash dill, dry with paper towel, and chop enough to measure 1 teaspoon. If using fresh Brussels sprouts, trim off bottoms and discolored leaves, wash, and drain.
2. Steam Brussels sprouts, 8 to 10 minutes, or until slightly crisp-tender. Set aside.
3. Heat butter in skillet until foaming. Stir dill into butter,

then add Brussels sprouts and walnuts and sauté over high heat about 2 minutes, stirring constantly, just until edges of walnuts begin to brown.
4. Add honey, stir to coat, and cook 4 to 5 minutes, stirring constantly, until honey just begins to caramelize.

Tomatoes Vinaigrette

1¼ teaspoons capers
Small bunch basil
½ teaspoon fennel seeds
1 small egg
½ cup olive oil
2 tablespoons red wine vinegar
Salt and freshly ground white pepper
8 leaves Bibb or leaf lettuce
4 sprigs watercress (optional)
2 medium-size tomatoes (about 1 pound total weight)
Medium-size green bell pepper

1. Rinse and drain capers; dry with paper towel and mince. Wash basil; dry with paper towel and chop enough to measure 1 teaspoon. Crush fennel seeds. Separate egg; place white in medium-size bowl, preferably stainless steel, and reserve yolk for another use.
2. To egg white add olive oil, vinegar, capers, basil, fennel seeds, and salt and pepper to taste. Whisk vigorously 10 to 15 seconds, or until mixture becomes slightly frothy. Add 1 to 2 tablespoons water, if desired, to reduce acidity.
3. Wash lettuce and watercress, if using, and dry with paper towels or in salad spinner; refrigerate in plastic bags. Wash tomatoes; cut into ¼-inch rounds. Wash, dry, core, halve, seed, and remove membranes from green pepper; cut into 2 x ¼-inch strips.
4. Place tomato slices and green pepper strips in shallow glass dish. Beat vinaigrette dressing to recombine; pour over vegetables. Cover dish and refrigerate for approximately 30 minutes.
5. Just before serving, divide lettuce leaves among 4 salad plates and top with sliced tomatoes and peppers. Garnish each serving with sprig of watercress, if desired.

LEFTOVER SUGGESTION

Since only the potato shells are used in the main-course recipe, use the rest of the potato flesh as a thickener for any light soup or for making vichyssoise.

Salmon Turbans with Béarnaise Sauce
Wild Rice with Pecans
Buttered Asparagus Spears

Remove any visible fat from the salmon before cooking because it will give the fish an undesirable flavor. If you cannot find fillets of the recommended size, buy smaller pieces and mold them to the sides of the ramekins.

The filling for the turbans is a mixture of chopped mushrooms, shallots, green pepper, and garlic. Wrap the chopped mushrooms in cheesecloth or a towel and wring out any excess moisture before sautéing.

If the Béarnaise sauce begins to separate or thin, remove it from the heat and continue to whisk to lower its

Eggs in rolled salmon fillets are topped with vegetables and a Béarnaise sauce for a dazzling dinner. The asparagus spears are delicately flavored with a thyme butter and the wild rice is tossed with pecans.

temperature. You might slowly add a few drops of cold water, milk, or cream to the sauce, then speed up whisking as soon as the eggs begin to accept the liquid.

WHAT TO DRINK

Choose a very dry, firm white wine such as an Alsatian Gewürztraminer or Riesling or a California Gewürztraminer or Sauvignon Blanc for this menu.

SHOPPING LIST AND STAPLES

Four ¾-inch-thick skinless salmon fillets (each about 5 ounces, measuring 2 x 6 inches), or Dover sole, lemon sole, or flounder

16 asparagus spears (about 1 pound total weight)
Small green bell pepper
2 ounces mushrooms
Small bunch fresh tarragon, or ½ teaspoon dried
2 large shallots
2 medium-size cloves garlic
Large lemon
7 large eggs
1 stick unsalted butter, plus 1 stick salted
2¼ cups chicken stock, preferably homemade (see page 13), or canned
2 tablespoons tarragon vinegar
¾ cup wild rice
3-ounce can pecan halves
Pinch of dried dill
Pinch of dried thyme, plus ½ teaspoon
Salt
2 peppercorns
Freshly ground white pepper
2 tablespoons dry white wine

UTENSILS

Medium-size heavy-gauge skillet
Small heavy-gauge skillet
2 medium-size heavy-gauge saucepans, 1 with cover
Small heavy-gauge saucepan
Double boiler or medium-size saucepan and stainless steel bowl
Vegetable steamer
Small bowl
Four 10- to 12-ounce ramekins or soufflé dishes
Colander
Fine sieve or cheesecloth
Measuring cups and spoons
Chef's knife
Paring knife
Wooden spoon
Rubber spatula
Whisk

START-TO-FINISH STEPS

1. Juice lemon to measure 2 tablespoons for salmon recipe, 1 teaspoon for Béarnaise recipe, and 1 tablespoon for asparagus recipe.
2. Follow wild rice recipe steps 1 through 3.
3. While rice is cooking, follow salmon recipe steps 1 through 3, asparagus recipe step 1, and Béarnaise recipe steps 1 through 6.
4. Follow wild rice recipe step 4 and salmon recipe steps 4 through 6.

5. While fish bakes, follow asparagus recipe steps 2 and 3, and wild rice recipe step 5.

6. Follow salmon recipe step 7 and asparagus recipe step 4.

7. Follow wild rice recipe step 6, Béarnaise recipe step 7, and serve with salmon turbans and buttered asparagus.

RECIPES

Salmon Turbans with Béarnaise Sauce

Four ¾-inch-thick skinless salmon fillets (each about 5 ounces, measuring 2 x 6 inches), or Dover sole, lemon sole, or flounder
Salt and freshly ground white pepper
Pinch of dried dill
Pinch of dried thyme
2 tablespoons lemon juice
4 tablespoons unsalted butter
2 ounces mushrooms
Small green bell pepper
2 medium-size cloves garlic
2 large shallots
4 large eggs
Béarnaise Sauce (see following recipe)

1. Preheat oven to 350 degrees.

2. Season salmon fillets with salt, pepper, dill, thyme, and lemon juice to taste.

3. Melt butter in medium-size heavy-gauge skillet. Lightly brush inside of ramekins or soufflé dishes with melted butter and curl fillets around insides of dishes; cover and set aside. Set aside skillet.

4. Wipe mushrooms with damp paper towel and dice finely to measure about ½ cup. Wash pepper; halve, seed, remove membranes, and dice finely to measure about ½ cup. Peel garlic and mince to measure about 2 teaspoons. Peel shallots and dice to measure about ¼ cup.

5. Set skillet with remaining butter over high heat. Add vegetables and sauté 3 to 4 minutes, stirring constantly, until shallots begin to brown. Remove from heat.

6. Break 1 egg into each salmon-lined ramekin. Spoon in one quarter of sautéed vegetables. Cover with foil and bake turbans 10 to 12 minutes, or until salmon flakes easily.

7. With rubber spatula, carefully turn each turban out onto a dinner plate and top with Béarnaise Sauce.

Béarnaise Sauce

Small bunch fresh tarragon, or ½ teaspoon dried
2 tablespoons tarragon vinegar
2 peppercorns
2 tablespoons dry white wine
1 stick salted butter
3 large eggs
1 teaspoon lemon juice

1. If using fresh tarragon, rinse gently, dry with paper towels, and chop enough to measure 1 tablespoon. Combine half the tarragon with tarragon vinegar, pepper-

corns, and white wine in small heavy-gauge saucepan. Boil over medium-high heat about 7 minutes, or until mixture is reduced by one half. Strain mixture through fine sieve or cheesecloth into small bowl.

2. In same saucepan, heat butter until foaming. Remove pan from heat; set aside.

3. Bring 1 to 2 inches water to a boil in bottom of double boiler or medium-size saucepan.

4. Separate eggs, reserving whites for another use. Place yolks and lemon juice in top of double boiler or in stainless steel bowl; set over simmering water. Whisk mixture vigorously to the consistency of heavy cream, about 4 to 5 minutes. (Keep water at a simmer; if eggs become too hot they will separate.)

5. Remove bowl from heat and, whisking constantly, add small amounts of melted butter alternately with drops of tarragon mixture, incorporating each addition completely.

6. Combine sauce and remaining tarragon; cover to keep warm until ready to use.

7. Just before serving, whisk to recombine sauce.

Wild Rice with Pecans

2¼ cups chicken stock
¾ cup wild rice
2 tablespoons unsalted butter
½ cup pecan halves

1. Bring stock to a simmer in medium-size saucepan over medium-high heat.

2. Wash wild rice under cold running water and drain.

3. Stir rice into hot chicken stock. Bring to a simmer, cover, and cook 35 minutes, or until rice is tender, stirring occasionally.

4. Drain any excess stock from rice; cover and set aside until ready to serve.

5. Melt butter in small skillet over medium-high heat. Add pecans, and sauté about 3 minutes, until edges of pecans begin to turn golden brown.

6. Just before serving, toss pecans with wild rice.

Buttered Asparagus Spears

16 asparagus spears (about 1 pound total weight)
½ teaspoon dried thyme
¼ teaspoon salt
Freshly ground white pepper
1 tablespoon lemon juice
2 tablespoons unsalted butter

1. Wash asparagus, trim off woody ends, and peel, if desired. Set aside.

2. Combine thyme, salt, pepper to taste, lemon juice, and butter in small heavy-gauge saucepan. Warm, stirring, over medium heat just until butter melts. Set aside.

3. Steam asparagus 3 to 4 minutes in vegetable steamer over boiling water just until crisp-tender.

4. Divide asparagus among plates and drizzle with butter sauce.

California Omelets
Snow Peas and Carrots Polonaise

Hearty omelets filled with chicken, peppers, and hearts of palm are accompanied by snow peas and carrots with a crumb topping.

Hearts of palm are a primary ingredient in these quick omelets. This delicious but expensive vegetable is taken from the cream-colored interior of small palm trees, usually palmettos. The hearts are like velvety white asparagus stalks in appearance and texture; they taste something like artichokes. Fresh hearts of palm are rare, but they are widely available canned at specialty food shops. Refrigerate leftovers in a nonmetal container filled with water.

The carrots and snow peas are prepared with a Polish-style topping that contains chopped hard-boiled eggs, fresh parsley, and bread crumbs sautéed in butter and garlic. Select snow peas, also known as Chinese pea pods, that are very crisp and bright green. Refrigerate the pods, unwashed, in a paper bag inside a plastic bag. If fresh snow peas are unavailable, use peeled broccoli stems or green beans.

WHAT TO DRINK

A medium-bodied dry white Alsatian or Italian Pinot Blanc would be good here. The cook also suggests a light red Beaujolais.

SHOPPING LIST AND STAPLES

2 whole chicken breasts (about 1 pound total weight), skinned and boned
2 medium-size carrots (about ½ pound total weight)
½ pound snow peas
4 medium-size hearts of palm, or 14-ounce can water-packed artichoke hearts
Large red bell pepper
Small bunch parsley
Small bunch scallions
3 small cloves garlic
9 large eggs
1 stick plus 1 to 4 tablespoons unsalted butter
2 ounces Parmesan cheese
2 ounces Gruyère cheese
3 to 4 slices stale bread
Salt and freshly ground white pepper

UTENSILS

Food processor (optional)
2 medium-size skillets
Omelet pan
Small saucepan
Vegetable steamer
9 x 13-inch heavy-gauge baking sheet
8 x 8-inch flameproof baking dish
Medium-size bowl
Wooden bowl and chopper (if not using processor)
Colander
Measuring cups and spoons
Chef's knife
Paring knife

Wooden spoon
Metal spatula
Whisk
Grater (if not using processor)
Vegetable peeler
Scissors

START-TO-FINISH STEPS

1. Peel garlic and mince to measure 2 teaspoons for omelets recipe and 1 teaspoon for snow peas and carrots. Trim scallions and wash; dry with paper towels and chop green parts to measure ¼ cup for omelets recipe. Wash parsley, dry with paper towels, and chop 1 tablespoon for garnish for omelets recipe and 1 tablespoon for snow peas and carrots recipe.
2. Prepare snow peas and carrots recipe steps 1 through 4.
3. Follow omelets recipe steps 1 through 12.
4. Follow snow peas and carrots recipe steps 5 through 7.
5. Follow omelets recipe step 13.
6. Follow snow peas and carrots recipe step 8.
7. Follow omelets recipe step 14, snow peas and carrots recipe step 9, and serve.

RECIPES

California Omelets

2 whole chicken breasts (about 1 pound total weight), skinned and boned
Salt
Freshly ground white pepper
Large red bell pepper
4 medium-size hearts of palm or artichoke hearts
6 tablespoons unsalted butter
2 teaspoons finely minced garlic
¼ cup finely chopped scallion greens
2 ounces Parmesan cheese
2 ounces Gruyère cheese
8 large eggs
1 tablespoon chopped fresh parsley for garnish

1. Cut chicken breasts into 2 x ¼-inch strips. Season with salt and pepper to taste.
2. Wash red pepper; halve, remove membranes, and seed. Slice each half into twelve ¼-inch strips.
3. Drain hearts of palm; dry with paper towels and slice into 2 x ¼-inch strips.
4. Melt 2 tablespoons butter in medium-size skillet. Add chicken breast strips and sauté about 5 minutes over medium-high heat, until lightly browned on all sides. Remove strips from pan and keep warm.
5. Reserve 12 strips of red pepper for garnish and add remainder to skillet along with garlic and scallions. Stirring constantly, cook over high heat about 4 minutes, until peppers are just crisp-tender. Set aside.
6. In food processor fitted with grating disk, or with cheese grater, grate cheeses to measure about ½ cup each; toss together.

7. Preheat oven to 200 degrees.

8. Beat eggs and ½ cup water in medium-size bowl. Season lightly with salt and pepper.

9. Melt 1 tablespoon butter in omelet pan over medium-high heat. When butter foams, make first of 4 omelets, using one quarter of egg mixture (see page 11). When omelet has set, in 40 to 60 seconds, remove from heat, and sprinkle with 1 teaspoon grated cheeses.

10. Lay one quarter of chicken breast strips down one half of omelet and top with one quarter of sautéed vegetables. With spatula, fold omelet in half, transfer to baking sheet, and set in oven to keep warm.

11. Repeat steps 9 and 10 for remaining omelets.

12. Remove omelets from oven. Adjust broiler rack to 4 inches from heat and turn oven to broil. Garnish each omelet with one quarter of the remaining cheese and red pepper strips.

13. Broil omelets 1 minute, or just until cheese has melted and begins to brown.

14. Transfer to plates and garnish with chopped parsley.

Snow Peas and Carrots Polonaise

1 large egg
2 medium-size carrots (about ½ pound total weight)
3 to 4 slices stale bread
3 to 6 tablespoons unsalted butter
1 teaspoon minced garlic
½ pound snow peas
1 tablespoon coarsely chopped fresh parsley

1. Boil egg 8 to 10 minutes, until very firm (see page 11).

2. Scrape carrots and cut diagonally into ¼-inch-thick slices.

3. Steam carrots 5 minutes, until barely cooked. Set aside.

4. Drain and peel egg; set aside.

5. Cube bread to measure 1½ cups. Melt 3 tablespoons butter in medium-size skillet, over medium-high heat. Sauté bread cubes and garlic, stirring frequently, adding more butter if necessary, about 3 minutes, until cubes are golden brown.

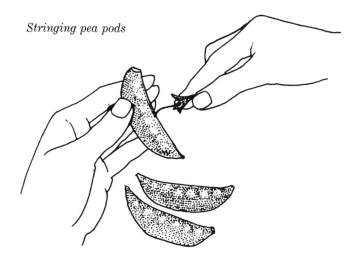

Stringing pea pods

6. String pea pods and trim ends (see preceding illustration). Wash and drain. Place sautéed bread cubes and garlic, hard-boiled egg, and parsley in food processor fitted with steel blade and process until egg and parsley are chopped and mixed with the bread crumbs; or chop in wooden bowl with chopper. Set aside.

7. Add snow peas to carrots in vegetable steamer. Steam 2 to 3 minutes, or just until crisp-tender.

8. Transfer vegetables to baking dish and top with bread crumb mixture. Place under preheated broiler 2 to 3 minutes, or until crumbs begin to brown.

9. Divide snow peas and carrots among 4 dinner plates, arranging portions so that crumbs are on top.

ADDED TOUCH

Serve these crunchy, deep-fried morsels as an appetizer while you finish preparing the omelets and vegetables.

Vegetable Fritters with Garlic Butter

1 tablespoon vegetable oil, plus additional for deep frying
1½ to 2 cups flour
½ cup buttermilk
4 large eggs, lightly beaten
½ cup stale beer
Freshly grated nutmeg
Salt
2 cups fennel in julienne strips, or 1 cup grated carrot
1 stick unsalted butter
4 teaspoons minced garlic
½ cup finely chopped scallions
½ cup grated Cheddar cheese

1. Combine 1 tablespoon vegetable oil, 1½ cups flour, buttermilk, eggs, beer, and nutmeg and salt to taste. Whisk thoroughly to blend ingredients. If batter seems thin (it should be the consistency of muffin batter), beat in a little more flour. Let batter stand 1 hour.

2. Steam fennel 4 to 6 minutes, until slightly undercooked. Transfer to platter, allow to cool slightly, and refrigerate.

3. Melt butter over medium heat until foaming. Add minced garlic, reduce heat to low, and cook, stirring occasionally, about 3 minutes. Remove from heat and let stand until serving time.

4. Stir steamed fennel, finely chopped scallions, and grated Cheddar cheese into batter.

5. Preheat oven to 200 degrees.

6. Heat oil for deep frying to 375 degrees on a deep fat thermometer.

7. Drop batter by heaping tablespoons into hot oil. Cook fritters, a few at a time, about 2 to 3 minutes, until golden brown.

8. Drain fritters on paper towels. Keep warm in oven while remaining fritters are cooked.

9. Strain garlic butter through fine sieve or cheesecloth. Set briefly over medium-high heat just to warm.

10. Remove fritters from oven and serve immediately accompanied by garlic butter.

Copeland Marks

MENU 1 (Right)
Zucchini and Coconut Milk Soup
Spicy Hard-Boiled Eggs
Indonesian Fried Rice

MENU 2
Shrimp, Tofu, and Tomato Omelets
Fried Rice Noodles
Cucumber and Bean Sprout Salad

MENU 3
Scrambled Eggs and Green Beans
with Hot Sauce
Plantain Purée

A dedicated food historian, Copeland Marks travels to remote regions of Asia, Central America, and North Africa to record their cuisines and culinary traditions, in particular, the cooking of Indonesia and Guatemala. Back in his New York kitchen, he re-creates the recipes he has collected, adapting them for American cooks.

Indonesian cuisine, richly spiced and often fiery with chilies, is based on garlic, ginger, coconut, rice, chicken, beef, and seafood. Copeland Marks presents two Indonesian-style meals for either lunch or dinner. Menu 1 features a zucchini and coconut milk soup and a traditional Indonesian egg dish—hard-boiled eggs browned in oil, then simmered in a spicy sauce. The accompanying stir-fried rice, with the addition of garlic, celery, watercress, and red pepper flakes, is quite different from Chinese stir-fried rice. In Menu 2 he offers a shrimp omelet, or *dadar udang*, stir-fried rice noodles, and a cucumber and bean sprout salad vinaigrette.

For a change of pace, Menu 3 features Mayan dishes from Guatemala: a traditional green bean and scrambled egg dish with hot sauce (*huevos revueltos con ejotes*), served with a tropical favorite, plantains.

Zucchini and coconut milk soup, flavored with dried shrimp, introduces this Indonesian meal. For the main course, hard-boiled eggs are served with a pungent sauce of red peppers, garlic, and red onion slices, accompanied by stir-fried rice. Garnish the plates with orange slices and sprigs of watercress.

Zucchini and Coconut Milk Soup
Spicy Hard-Boiled Eggs
Indonesian Fried Rice

The richly seasoned zucchini and coconut milk soup from Java contains two traditional Indonesian ingredients—coconut milk and dried shrimp, which are optional. Sold in cellophane bags wherever Asian ingredients are available, dried shrimp keep for 6 months stored in an airtight jar or indefinitely in the freezer.

Freshly made coconut milk is preferable to the canned variety, if you have the time. Discard the water from a fresh coconut and grate enough meat to measure 1 cup. Put it into a blender or food processor and add 1 cup of boiling water. If substituting packaged unsweetened shredded coconut for fresh, use boiling milk in place of water. Blend for 2 minutes, then let the mixture steep for 15 to 30 minutes. Pour the mixture through a fine strainer, pressing out as much liquid from the coconut as possible. Reserve this liquid, or "milk"; discard the pulp. As the "milk" cools, a thickened cream will rise to the surface; recombine it with the "milk." Coconut milk is highly perishable, so use it immediately, or store it in the freezer.

WHAT TO DRINK

With this spicy menu, try a light and slightly sweet German white wine such as a Moselle.

SHOPPING LIST AND STAPLES

4-ounce package dried shrimp (optional)
4 medium-size zucchini (about 2 pounds total weight)
Large red bell pepper
Small white or yellow onion
Medium-size red onion
Small bunch celery with leaves
Small bunch scallions
Small bunch watercress
4 medium-size cloves garlic
Large lemon
Medium-size orange
9 large eggs
15-ounce can unsweetened coconut milk, preferably from Thailand, or 2 cups fresh (see above)
6 tablespoons corn or peanut oil
3 tablespoons Chinese soy sauce
1 cup long-grain white rice
2½ teaspoons sugar
2 teaspoons red pepper flakes
Salt and freshly ground white pepper

UTENSILS

Large skillet or wok
Large sauté pan with cover
2 medium-size saucepans, 1 heavy-gauge with cover
Baking sheet
Large bowl
Medium-size bowl
2 small bowls
Salad spinner (optional)
Large strainer
Measuring cups and spoons
Chef's knife
Paring knife
Metal fork
Wok spatula (if using wok)
Rubber spatula
Ladle

START-TO-FINISH STEPS

The night before: Follow rice recipe steps 1 through 4.

One hour ahead: If preparing homemade coconut milk for soup recipe, follow directions given above.

1. Prepare onions and garlic; set aside.
2. Follow eggs recipe steps 1 through 3.
3. While eggs are cooking, rinse lemon and dry with paper towel. Cut lemon in half and squeeze, reserving 4 tablespoons juice for eggs recipe. Cut juiced lemon halves into 1-inch-square pieces, removing as much flesh and white pith as possible; reserve lemon peel for soup recipe.
4. Follow eggs recipe step 4 and rice recipe steps 5 through 7.
5. Follow eggs recipe steps 5 and 6 and soup recipe step 1.
6. Follow eggs recipe steps 7 and 8 and rice recipe steps 8 through 10.
7. Follow soup recipe steps 2 through 4, and serve.
8. Follow eggs recipe step 9, rice recipe step 11, and serve.

RECIPES

Zucchini and Coconut Milk Soup

4 medium-size zucchini (about 2 pounds total weight)
½ cup thinly sliced white or yellow onion
2 medium-size cloves garlic, thinly sliced
Freshly ground white pepper

4 one-inch-square pieces lemon peel
1 teaspoon salt
¼ cup dried shrimp (optional)
2 cups canned unsweetened coconut milk, preferably from Thailand, or 2 cups fresh, at room temperature

1. Rinse zucchini, dry with paper towel, and trim off ends. Cut in half lengthwise, then cut each half crosswise into ½-inch-thick slices.
2. Combine onion, garlic, pepper, lemon peel, salt, and shrimp, if using, with 1 cup water in medium-size saucepan. Bring to a boil over medium heat and boil gently 2 minutes.
3. Add zucchini to pan and reduce heat to medium-low. Stir in coconut milk. Simmer soup, stirring occasionally, until squash is just tender, about 5 minutes.
4. Ladle soup into individual bowls and serve.

Spicy Hard-Boiled Eggs

8 large eggs
Large red bell pepper
3 tablespoons corn or peanut oil
¼ cup thinly sliced red onion
1 medium-size clove garlic, chopped
1 teaspoon red pepper flakes
¾ teaspoon salt
1 teaspoon sugar
4 tablespoons lemon juice

1. Preheat oven to 200 degrees.
2. Place eggs in medium-size saucepan with enough cold water to cover and bring to a boil over medium-high heat. Reduce heat and simmer eggs 8 to 10 minutes.
3. Meanwhile, rinse red bell pepper and dry with paper towel. Core, halve, seed, and finely chop enough pepper to measure 1 cup.
4. To test eggs for doneness, remove one from pan, and lightly crack shell. Under cold running water, peel off just enough shell to check that egg white is firm. If done, immediately drain hot water from eggs and fill pan with cold water. Remove eggs from pan and peel, then rinse under cold running water and dry with paper towels.
5. Heat oil in large sauté pan over medium heat. Add eggs and sauté, shaking pan gently, until they are lightly browned, about 3 minutes. Transfer eggs to medium-size bowl.
6. Add red onion, garlic, and chopped pepper to pan, and stir fry over medium heat 2 minutes. Stir in red pepper flakes, salt, sugar, lemon juice, and ½ cup water, and bring to a simmer. Reduce heat to low and cook mixture, stirring occasionally, until thickened, about 5 minutes.
7. Return eggs to pan and raise heat to medium. Return sauce to a simmer and cook 5 minutes, stirring occasionally, until eggs are heated through.
8. Turn off heat under pan and remove eggs. Cover pan to keep sauce warm. Cut eggs in half lengthwise and divide among plates. Place in oven to keep warm.

9. When ready to serve, top each serving of eggs with a spoonful of sauce.

Indonesian Fried Rice

1 cup long-grain white rice
1 large egg
3 tablespoons Chinese soy sauce
1½ teaspoons sugar
2 to 3 scallions
1 stalk celery with leaves
Small bunch watercress
1 medium-size orange for garnish (optional)
3 tablespoons corn or peanut oil
½ cup thinly sliced red onion
1 clove garlic, thinly sliced
1 teaspoon red pepper flakes

1. Place rice in large bowl with enough cold water to cover. With your hand, stir 15 to 20 seconds. Drain rice in strainer; dry bowl.
2. Transfer rice to medium-size heavy-gauge saucepan. Add 1¾ cups water to pan and bring to a rolling boil over medium-high heat. When bubbles climb nearly to rim of pan, in about 30 seconds, cover and reduce heat to maintain a gentle simmer. Cook rice 15 minutes without lifting cover. Remove pan from heat and let rest, covered, 20 minutes.
3. Remove cover and gently fluff rice with fork to separate grains. Spread rice in thin layer on baking sheet to cool.
4. When thoroughly cool, transfer to large bowl used for soaking, cover with plastic wrap, and refrigerate until needed.
5. Beat egg in small bowl and set aside. In another small bowl, combine soy sauce with sugar and stir until blended; set aside.
6. Wash scallions and dry with paper towels. Trim off ends and chop enough white and green parts to measure ¼ cup. Wash celery, dry, and thinly slice enough leaves to measure about ¼ cup. Reserve stalks for another use.
7. Wash watercress and dry in salad spinner or pat dry with paper towels. Reserve 4 sprigs for garnish, if desired. Trim and discard stems from remaining watercress and chop enough to measure ½ cup; set aside. If using orange for garnish, rinse and dry with paper towel. Cut orange into ¼-inch-thick slices and remove seeds. Cut slices in half and set aside.
8. Heat oil in large skillet or wok over medium-high heat. Add red onion, garlic, and red pepper flakes, and stir fry 1 minute. Add chilled rice and stir with wooden fork to separate grains. Add scallions, celery leaves, and watercress, and stir fry until ingredients are combined and onions and scallions are crisp-tender, about 3 minutes.
9. Add soy mixture to pan and stir fry 1 minute. Add beaten egg and stir fry until rice is coated with egg and egg is set, about another 2 minutes.
10. Divide among 4 plates and keep warm in oven.
11. Just before serving, garnish plates with watercress sprigs and orange slices, if desired.

Shrimp, Tofu, and Tomato Omelets
Fried Rice Noodles
Cucumber and Bean Sprout Salad

The omelets of shrimp, tofu, and tomato; the rice noodles stir-fried with chicken and Asian seasonings; and the bean sprout salad topped with hard-boiled eggs and roasted peanuts provide an appealing interplay of textures.

Ivory-colored bean curd—or tofu—is a primary ingredient in the main-course shrimp omelet. This protein-rich soybean product is available in many textures, ranging from semi-liquid to firm. For this omelet recipe, use firm tofu because it retains its shape when cubed.

WHAT TO DRINK

A Riesling from Germany, Washington, Oregon, or New York State would be excellent with this light meal.

SHOPPING LIST AND STAPLES

¾ pound medium-size shrimp
1 skinless, boneless chicken breast (about 6 ounces)
2 cups bean sprouts
4 ounces firm tofu
Small tomato
Medium-size cucumber
Large red bell pepper
Small green bell pepper
Medium-size onion
Small bunch scallions
2 large cloves garlic
Small head red leaf lettuce
7 large eggs
¼ cup plus 3 tablespoons corn or peanut oil
1 teaspoon sesame oil
¼ cup cider vinegar
3 tablespoons Chinese soy sauce
½ pound Chinese rice noodles *(maifun)*
2½ teaspoons sugar
4-ounce can dry-roasted peanuts
1 teaspoon red pepper flakes
Salt and freshly ground pepper

UTENSILS

2 large skillets or 1 large skillet and 1 wok
Nonstick or well-seasoned omelet pan or small
    heavy-gauge skillet
Large saucepan
Medium-size saucepan
Large heatproof bowl
2 medium-size bowls
2 small bowls
Colander

Salad spinner (optional)
Measuring cups and spoons
Chef's knife
Paring knife
Slotted spoon
Wooden spoon
Vinyl spatula (if using nonstick omelet pan) or
    metal spatula
Rubber spatula
Whisk

START-TO-FINISH STEPS

1. Prepare vegetables for omelets, noodles, and salad.
2. Follow omelets recipe steps 1 and 2.
3. Follow salad recipe steps 1 through 4.
4. Follow omelets recipe steps 3 through 5.
5. Follow noodles recipe steps 1 through 5.
6. Follow omelets recipe steps 6 through 8.
7. Follow salad recipe step 5, omelets recipe step 9, and serve with noodles.

RECIPES

Shrimp, Tofu, and Tomato Omelets

4 ounces firm tofu, cut into 12 bite-size pieces
Salt
Small tomato
¾ pound medium-size shrimp
6 large eggs
¼ cup corn or peanut oil, approximately
⅓ cup thinly sliced onion
½ teaspoon chopped garlic
Freshly ground pepper

1. Preheat oven to 200 degrees.
2. Place tofu on paper towels and press to absorb moisture.
3. In medium-size saucepan, bring 2 quarts water and 2 teaspoons salt to a boil over high heat. Blanch tomato 15 seconds. Peel, seed, and chop coarsely; set aside.
4. Add shrimp to boiling water in pan and cook just until they turn bright orange-pink, 2 to 3 minutes.
5. Immediately drain shrimp in colander and refresh under cold water. Peel, devein, and cut shrimp into bite-size pieces, reserving 4 whole shrimp for garnish.
6. In medium-size bowl, whisk eggs until well blended.
7. Heat 2 tablespoons oil in large skillet over medium heat. Add onion, garlic, and tofu, and sauté, stirring occasionally, until mixture turns golden, about 3 minutes. Add cut-up and whole shrimp and salt and pepper to taste; stir fry 2 minutes. Remove whole shrimp from pan; set aside. Remove skillet from heat.
8. Lightly coat the bottom of a nonstick or well-seasoned omelet pan with oil and place over medium heat. Transfer one quarter of shrimp-tofu mixture to pan and distribute evenly over bottom. Pour one quarter of eggs over mixture, tilting pan to distribute evenly, and allow to set 3 minutes. Turn omelet over with spatula and cook another

2 minutes. Fold in half, turn onto dinner plate, and place in oven. Repeat for each omelet.
9. Garnish each omelet with 1 whole shrimp and parsley sprig, if desired.

Fried Rice Noodles

½ pound Chinese rice noodles (*maifun*)
Small bunch scallions
1 skinless, boneless chicken breast (about 6 ounces)
3 tablespoons Chinese soy sauce
1½ teaspoons sugar
3 tablespoons corn or peanut oil
¼ cup thinly sliced onion
¼ cup thinly sliced green pepper
2 teaspoons finely chopped garlic
1 teaspoon red pepper flakes

1. In large heatproof bowl, soak noodles in 2 quarts boiling water for 10 minutes.
2. Rinse scallions, dry with paper towels, and cut green parts into ¼-inch pieces. Cut chicken into bite-size pieces. In small bowl, combine soy sauce and sugar.
3. Turn noodles into colander and drain; dry bowl.
4. Heat oil in large skillet or wok over medium-high heat. Add chicken and stir fry 2 minutes. Add scallions, onion, green pepper, garlic, and pepper flakes, and stir fry 2 minutes. Add noodles, stir fry another 2 minutes.
5. Add sweetened soy sauce to noodles and stir fry another 2 minutes, or until chicken is heated through. Turn noodles into large dry bowl, cover loosely with foil, and keep warm in 200-degree oven.

Cucumber and Bean Sprout Salad

Small head red leaf lettuce
2 cups bean sprouts
1 large hard-boiled egg
¼ cup cider vinegar
1 teaspoon sugar
¼ teaspoon salt
½ cup peeled, diced cucumber
1 cup red bell pepper, cut in ½-inch dice
1 teaspoon sesame oil
2 tablespoons dry-roasted peanuts

1. Wash lettuce and dry in salad spinner or dry with paper towels; separate leaves and refrigerate.
2. In medium-size saucepan, bring 1 quart of water to a boil over medium-high heat. Add bean sprouts and blanch 2 minutes. Turn sprouts into colander and refresh under cold water. Transfer to paper towels and dry.
3. Peel egg. Mash with fork in small bowl and set aside.
4. In another small bowl, blend vinegar, sugar, and salt. In medium-size bowl, combine bean sprouts, diced cucumber, and diced pepper. Add sesame oil and toss. Add vinegar mixture and toss again to combine. Cover bowl with plastic wrap and refrigerate.
5. Divide lettuce among 4 dinner plates, top with bean sprout mixture, and sprinkle with egg and peanuts.

Scrambled Eggs and Green Beans with Hot Sauce
Plantain Purée

For a traditional Guatemalan meal, serve eggs scrambled with green beans and tomatoes, hot sauce, and a plantain purée.

The plantain purée is a hearty dish that offsets the scrambled eggs with hot sauce. Plantains are large, thick-skinned, yellowish-green bananas. They have a mild flavor similar to that of squash. To be edible, they must be cooked. Buy plantains that are partially ripe, with yellow-black skins. If plantains are not available, substitute sweet potatoes. Boil cut-up, unpeeled sweet potatoes until fork-tender, about 25 to 30 minutes. Then peel and purée them as you would the plantains.

WHAT TO DRINK

This menu calls for ice-cold beer—preferably a dark, full-bodied brand from Japan or Mexico.

SHOPPING LIST AND STAPLES

2 large semi-ripe plantains or 1 pound sweet potatoes
16-ounce can whole tomatoes
½ pound green beans
Small onion
Small bunch scallions
Medium-size clove garlic
Small bunch parsley for garnish (optional)
8 large eggs
½ pint sour cream
1 tablespoon unsalted butter
5 tablespoons corn or peanut oil
1 tablespoon honey

Pinch of cinnamon
Freshly grated or ground nutmeg
2 to 3 teaspoons red pepper flakes, or 1 small hot
   fresh green chili
Salt and freshly ground pepper

UTENSILS

Food processor or blender
Large skillet
1 medium-size skillet with cover
2 medium-size saucepans
Small saucepan with cover
2 medium-size bowls, 1 ovenproof
Colander
Salad spinner (optional)
Measuring cups and spoons
Chef's knife
Paring knife
Wooden spoon
Wooden spatula
Rubber spatula
Whisk
Nutmeg grater (optional)
Rubber gloves (if using fresh chili)

START-TO-FINISH STEPS

1. Prepare onions and tomatoes for eggs recipe and for hot sauce recipe.
2. Follow plantain recipe steps 1 through 3.
3. Follow hot sauce recipe steps 1 through 4. Wash processor or blender for plantains.
4. While hot sauce cooks, follow plantain recipe step 4.
5. Follow eggs recipe steps 1 through 6, plantain recipe step 5, and serve with hot sauce.

RECIPES

Scrambled Eggs and Green Beans with Hot Sauce

½ pound green beans
Salt
3 tablespoons corn or peanut oil
¼ cup thinly sliced onion
½ cup thinly sliced scallions
¼ cup seeded, chopped, canned tomatoes, drained
Freshly ground pepper
8 large eggs
Hot Sauce (see following recipe)
8 parsley sprigs for garnish (optional)

1. Place 4 dinner plates in 200-degree oven to warm.
2. Wash beans thoroughly and snap off ends; set aside.
3. In medium-size saucepan, bring 2 cups water and ½ teaspoon salt to a boil. Add beans and cook 2 minutes. Transfer beans to colander, refresh under cold running water, and drain. Cut beans into ¼-inch pieces.

4. Heat oil in large skillet over medium heat. Add onions and scallions, and sauté, stirring occasionally, 2 minutes. Add tomatoes, beans, 1 teaspoon salt, and pepper to taste; stir fry 3 minutes more, or until beans are crisp-tender. Remove from heat.
5. In medium-size bowl, whisk eggs until well blended; add to bean mixture in skillet. Stir eggs with wooden spatula to combine with vegetables; cook 3 to 4 minutes over medium heat, until mixture is firm but creamy.
6. Divide mixture among warm dinner plates, top with hot sauce, and garnish each plate with 2 sprigs parsley, if desired.

Hot Sauce

Medium-size clove garlic
2 to 3 teaspoons red pepper flakes, or 1 small hot green
   fresh chili
1 cup seeded, chopped tomatoes, or 1 cup canned, drained
½ teaspoon salt
2 tablespoons corn or peanut oil
¼ cup chopped onion

1. Peel and chop enough garlic to measure 2 teaspoons. If using fresh chili, rinse and dry. Wearing thin rubber gloves, split in half, seed, chop finely, and set aside.
2. Combine tomatoes, garlic, salt, red pepper flakes, or chili, if using, and 1 cup water in small saucepan. Cover and cook over medium heat 10 minutes.
3. In medium-size skillet, heat oil over medium heat. Add onion and sauté, stirring occasionally, 2 minutes. Remove from heat.
4. Place tomato mixture in food processor fitted with steel blade or in blender and purée. Add purée to onion in skillet and simmer gently over low heat until sauce thickens, about 10 minutes. Cover skillet and set aside.

Plantain Purée

Salt
2 large semi-ripe plantains, or 1 pound sweet potatoes
1 tablespoon unsalted butter
1 tablespoon honey
Pinch of cinnamon
Freshly grated or ground nutmeg
1 cup sour cream

1. Preheat oven to 200 degrees.
2. Place 2 cups water and ¼ teaspoon salt in medium-size saucepan and bring to a boil over medium heat.
3. Without removing peel, cut each plantain into 4 pieces. Place plantains in boiling water and cook until just soft enough for tip of a sharp knife to penetrate skin easily, about 8 minutes. Transfer to colander; set aside.
4. Peel plantains and place in food processor fitted with steel blade, or blender. Add butter, honey, cinnamon and nutmeg; coarsely purée plantains. Place in medium-size ovenproof bowl, cover with foil, and keep warm in oven.
5. Divide purée among 4 small serving dishes. Garnish each with ¼ cup sour cream and sprinkle with additional nutmeg, if desired.

Ann Cashion

MENU 1 (Left)
Italian Pea Soufflés with Shrimp and Peppers
Cauliflower Parmesan

MENU 2
Eggs Florentine Tart
Warm Potato Salad with Tomatoes,
Bacon, and Rosemary

MENU 3
Two Pea Soup
Puffy Apple and Onion Omelets
Carrot and Bacon Gratin

Ann Cashion says that what has influenced her cooking most was the time she spent in Florence, Italy, where she was struck by the simplicity of Tuscan food and its meticulous preparation. In that spirit, she presents two Italian-style meals that use ingredients at their seasonal peak and emphasize natural flavors. Menu 1 features miniature Italian soufflés, or *sformati*, made here with fresh peas. Jumbo shrimp and roasted red pepper strips are arranged over the unmolded soufflés just before serving and golden cauliflower gratin accompanies the egg dish. In Menu 2, she serves an elegant brunch of eggs Florentine—fried eggs with creamed spinach—baked in an unsweetened tart shell. Boiled new potatoes, tomatoes, and *pancetta* (unsmoked Italian-style bacon rolled into a sausage shape) are combined in the warm side salad.

If Italian cooking is Ann Cashion's primary inspiration, the cuisine of California is certainly her secondary one. From her years as a cook in various restaurants on the West Coast, she learned that unusual combinations of ingredients within a dish, or in a succession of dishes, may contrast with and yet complement each other. Thus her first-course soup in Menu 3 mixes the unlikely flavors of split peas and snow peas, and the main-course omelets blend the sweetness of apples with the flavor of onions. The gratin of carrots and bacon has a hint of nutmeg.

A lavish portion of jumbo shrimp enhances these Italian pea soufflés, which are also topped with roasted red peppers and garlic-scented lemon butter. Serve a portion of the cauliflower Parmesan on the same plate and garnish each serving with a lemon wedge, cherry tomato, and scallion plumes.

Italian Pea Soufflés with Shrimp and Peppers
Cauliflower Parmesan

Egg yolks, puréed peas, and egg whites are folded into the basic white sauce of butter, milk, and flour, or *béchamel*, for these individual soufflés. Setting the soufflé dishes in a water bath gives the soufflés a dense, smooth consistency.

Select the head of cauliflower carefully. It should be white to creamy white, compact, and firm. Any dark brown specks on the surface mean that the head is old. Wrap the cauliflower in a perforated plastic bag and refrigerate, but use it quickly to prevent deterioration. To prepare the cauliflower for cooking, rinse it thoroughly, then pare away the outer leaves and stem.

WHAT TO DRINK

This meal needs a full-bodied white wine; choose a California Chardonnay or a white Mâcon or Saint-Véran.

SHOPPING LIST

16 jumbo unshelled shrimp, heads removed (about 1½ pounds total weight)
2 pounds fresh peas, preferably, or two 10-ounce packages frozen
Large head cauliflower
2 medium-size red bell peppers (about ½ pound total weight)
Small onion
1 pint cherry tomatoes (optional)
Small bunch scallions (optional)
Large clove garlic
2 lemons plus 1 for garnish (optional)
2 large eggs
⅔ cup milk
1 stick plus 4 tablespoons unsalted butter, approximately
¼ pound Parmesan cheese
2 tablespoons flour
Salt
Freshly ground pepper

UTENSILS

Food processor or food mill
Electric mixer
Large saucepan
Medium-size saucepan with cover
Small saucepan
17 x 11-inch roasting pan
13 x 9-inch flameproof baking dish
12-inch gratin dish
Four 1- to 1½-cup soufflé molds or ovenproof ramekins
Medium-size bowl
Small bowl
Colander
Large strainer
Measuring cups and spoons
Chef's knife
Paring knife
Wooden spoon
Rubber spatula
Grater
Juicer
Whisk
Metal tongs
Plastic or paper bag

START-TO-FINISH STEPS

At least 1 hour ahead: If using frozen peas for soufflés, set out to thaw.

1. Follow soufflés recipe steps 1 through 8.
2. While soufflés are baking, follow cauliflower recipe steps 1 through 3.
3. While cauliflower is cooking, follow soufflés recipe step 9.
4. While peppers are steaming, follow cauliflower recipe steps 4 and 5.
5. Follow soufflés recipe step 10 and cauliflower recipe step 6.
6. Follow soufflés recipe steps 11 through 14 and serve with cauliflower.

RECIPES

Italian Pea Soufflés with Shrimp and Peppers

2 pounds fresh peas, preferably, or two 10-ounce packages frozen, thawed
2 large eggs
Small onion
Large clove garlic
2 lemons plus 1 for garnish (optional)
4 scallions (optional)
4 cherry tomatoes (optional)

6 tablespoons unsalted butter, approximately
Salt and freshly ground pepper
2 tablespoons flour
⅔ cup milk
2 medium-size red bell peppers (about ½ pound total weight)
16 jumbo unshelled shrimp, heads removed (about 1½ pounds total weight)

1. Fill roasting pan with 1-inch water and place on lower rack in oven; place 1 rack at top. Preheat oven to 425 degrees.
2. If using fresh peas, shell enough to measure 2½ cups. In medium-size saucepan, bring 6 cups water and 1½ teaspoons salt to a boil over medium-high heat. Add peas and cook until tender, 5 to 7 minutes. If using frozen peas, follow package directions.
3. While peas are cooking, separate eggs, placing yolks in small bowl and whites in medium-size bowl. Peel and finely chop enough onion to measure 3 tablespoons. Peel and mince garlic to measure 1 tablespoon. Squeeze juice of 2 lemons and set aside.
4. Prepare garnishes, if using: Rinse lemon, scallions, and cherry tomatoes and dry with paper towels. Cut lemon into quarters. Trim scallions and make a 1-inch lengthwise cut at the root ends. Stem tomatoes.
5. In small saucepan, melt 3 tablespoons butter over medium heat. Add onion and sauté until tender but not browned, about 3 minutes. Add salt and pepper to taste, sprinkle onion with flour, and cook, stirring to blend, 1 minute, without allowing flour to brown. Raise heat to medium-high, slowly pour in milk, whisking constantly, until sauce boils. Remove from heat and add additional salt and pepper, if desired.
6. Drain peas in large strainer. Place in food processor fitted with steel blade and purée. Or put peas through food mill fitted with fine disk.
7. Add pea purée and egg yolks to white sauce, whisking to blend.
8. Gently fold egg whites into pea mixture with rubber spatula. Divide mixture among 4 soufflé molds or ramekins. Place molds in roasting pan and bake until puffed and browned, about 20 minutes. Wash and dry saucepan.
9. Meanwhile, roast red peppers. Turn 2 front burners of gas stove to high. Set 1 pepper directly on each grate. Watch closely and, as skin blackens in flame, turn peppers

with metal tongs until entire surface is black. Put peppers into paper bag and close; set aside to steam about 5 minutes.
10. Peel shrimp; with paring knife, slit down backs and lift out black veins, leaving tail shells intact.
11. Remove peppers from bag. Under running water, scrape away all blackened skin of peppers with paring knife. Core and halve peppers; remove seeds and membranes, and blot dry with paper towels. Cut peppers into julienne strips and combine with shrimp in flameproof baking dish.
12. In saucepan, melt remaining 3 tablespoons butter with minced garlic. Pour garlic butter and reserved lemon juice over shrimp. Lightly salt shrimp to taste and pepper generously.
13. Carefully remove roasting pan from oven, remove soufflés, and set aside. Place shrimp dish in water bath. Turn oven temperature to broil and set broiler rack 4 inches from heat. Broil shrimp and peppers about 5 minutes, turning once.
14. Run knife around edges of soufflés and turn out onto individual dinner plates. Top each soufflé with shrimp and peppers and a spoonful of pan juices. Garnish each plate with a lemon wedge, cherry tomato, and 2 scallions, if desired, and serve.

Cauliflower Parmesan

¼ pound Parmesan cheese
Salt
Large head cauliflower
Freshly ground pepper
6 tablespoons unsalted butter, approximately

1. Grate enough Parmesan to measure ¾ cup. Butter gratin dish well.
2. In large saucepan, bring 2 quarts water and 2 teaspoons salt to a boil over medium-high heat.
3. Wash cauliflower and separate head into enough florets to measure 3 cups. Place florets in pan and boil just until tender, 3 to 5 minutes.
4. Drain cauliflower in colander. Place florets, stem-side down, in gratin dish and add salt and pepper to taste. Sprinkle with Parmesan and dot with butter.
5. Place dish on top rack of 425-degree oven until cheese melts and begins to brown, about 5 to 7 minutes.
6. Remove cauliflower from oven and cover loosely with foil to keep warm.

Eggs Florentine Tart
Warm Potato Salad with Tomatoes, Bacon, and Rosemary

Paired with warm herbed potato salad, this handsome egg-topped tart makes an impressive buffet lunch or supper.

The main-course tart is filled with chopped spinach and grated Parmesan cheese in a white sauce. Be sure to squeeze as much cooking water as possible out of the spinach, or it may cause the filling to be runny.

The salad of new potatoes, tomatoes, and *pancetta* should *not* be chilled. Buy *pancetta* at an Italian meat market or specialty food shop. If you cannot find it, substitute lean bacon.

WHAT TO DRINK

A Soave or Pinot Grigio would be a good match for this Italian menu.

SHOPPING LIST AND STAPLES

½ pound pancetta or American bacon
16 new potatoes (about 2 pounds total weight)
2 medium-size cloves garlic
Small bunch fresh rosemary, or 1½ teaspoons dried
5 large eggs
1 cup milk
½ pint heavy cream
1 stick plus 6 tablespoons unsalted butter, approximately
2 ounces Parmesan cheese
10-ounce package frozen spinach, or 1½ pounds fresh
1-pound can crushed tomatoes
¼ cup virgin olive oil, approximately
2 tablespoons red wine vinegar
1½ cups all-purpose flour
Freshly grated nutmeg
Salt and freshly ground pepper

UTENSILS

Food processor
2 medium-size skillets
Large saucepan
2 medium-size saucepans, 1 heavy-gauge
Small saucepan
10-inch tart pan with removable bottom
Large bowl
Medium-size bowl
Small bowl
Colander
2 strainers, 1 coarse and 1 fine mesh
Measuring cups and spoons
Chef's knife

Paring knife
Wooden spoon
Rubber spatula
Grater
Whisk
Rolling pin
Pastry blender (optional)

START-TO-FINISH STEPS

At least 1 hour ahead of time: If using frozen spinach for tart filling, set out to thaw. Follow tart recipe steps 1 through 3.

1. Follow tart recipe steps 4 through 6.
2. While tart shell is baking, follow salad recipe steps 1 and 2.
3. Follow tart recipe steps 7 through 12.
4. Follow salad recipe steps 3 through 6.
5. Follow tart recipe steps 13 and 14.
6. Follow salad recipe step 7 and tart recipe step 15.
7. Follow salad recipe step 8, tart recipe step 16, and serve.

RECIPES

Eggs Florentine Tart

The tart shell:
1 large egg
6 tablespoons unsalted butter, chilled
1¼ cups all-purpose flour
Salt

The filling:
1 cup milk
1 cup heavy cream
7½ tablespoons unsalted butter
¼ cup flour
Salt and freshly ground pepper
Freshly grated nutmeg
10-ounce package frozen spinach, thawed, or 1½ pounds fresh
⅓ cup freshly grated Parmesan cheese
4 large eggs

1. Separate egg, placing yolk in small bowl and reserving white for another use. Cut butter into small pieces.
2. Combine flour, a scant ¾ teaspoon salt, and butter in

food processor fitted with steel blade. Blend, pulsing machine on and off, just until mixture resembles coarse cornmeal. Or, working quickly, blend mixture together with pastry blender or fingers.

3. Whisk 3 tablespoons cold water into egg yolk and add to flour mixture. Process briefly until mixture forms a paste. Or, beat in egg mixture with wooden spoon. Form dough into ball, wrap in waxed paper, and refrigerate at least 1 hour, or until ready to use.

4. Preheat oven to 425 degrees.

5. On well-floured surface, roll out dough into 13-inch circle. Fit pastry into 10-inch tart pan, gently pressing flat against bottom and sides; pastry will extend about ¾ inch over rim. Fold overhanging pastry back into pan, pressing against inside of rim all around to seal. Using your thumb, press pastry flush with pan rim.

6. With fork, lightly prick tart shell 8 to 10 times and bake until golden brown, about 12 minutes.

7. Remove tart shell from oven and allow to cool on rack at least 10 minutes, or until ready to use. Reduce oven temperature to 200 degrees.

8. Heat milk and cream in small saucepan over medium heat.

9. Meanwhile, melt 6 tablespoons butter in medium-size heavy-gauge saucepan over medium-low heat. When butter bubbles, add flour, salt, and pepper and nutmeg to taste, whisking until completely incorporated. Allow mixture to bubble 1 minute, being careful not to let it brown.

10. Add hot milk and cream, whisking constantly, and bring sauce to a boil. Reduce heat to very low and cook sauce, stirring occasionally, 30 to 45 minutes.

11. Cook spinach according to package directions. Or, if using fresh spinach, remove stems and discard. Wash thoroughly under cold running water; do not dry. Transfer to medium-size saucepan and steam over medium heat 2 minutes, or until wilted.

12. Turn spinach into strainer and refresh under cold running water; squeeze out as much moisture as possible with the back of a spoon. Finely chop spinach and transfer to medium-size saucepan; set aside.

13. Strain sauce through fine strainer into spinach. Stir in Parmesan and heat mixture over low heat, stirring, 4 to 5 minutes, or just until hot. Season with salt and pepper to taste; add more Parmesan, if desired.

14. Before filling tart shell, gently push bottom of pan up to free pastry from sides. Spoon spinach mixture into shell and keep warm in oven.

15. Over medium heat, melt remaining 1½ tablespoons butter in medium-size skillet until it begins to foam. Carefully break 4 eggs into skillet and cook, sunny-side up.

16. When whites are firm with yolks still runny, arrange eggs, overlapping edges of whites, on top of spinach in shell. Serve immediately.

Warm Potato Salad with Tomatoes, Bacon, and Rosemary

Salt
16 new potatoes (about 2 pounds total weight)
Large sprig rosemary, or 1½ teaspoons dried
¼ cup virgin olive oil, approximately
1-pound can crushed tomatoes, drained
2 medium-size cloves garlic, peeled and
   chopped
Freshly ground pepper
½ pound pancetta or American bacon
2 tablespoons red wine vinegar

1. Bring 2 quarts water and 2 teaspoons salt to a boil in large saucepan over high heat.

2. Meanwhile, wash potatoes, but do not peel; drain in colander. If using fresh rosemary, rinse and pat dry with paper towels. Finely chop enough rosemary to measure 2 tablespoons. If using dried, crush between 2 sheets of waxed paper with a rolling pin.

3. Place potatoes in boiling water and cook until knife inserted in center penetrates easily, 15 to 20 minutes.

4. While potatoes are boiling, heat 2 tablespoons olive oil in medium-size skillet over medium heat. Add drained tomatoes, rosemary, garlic, and salt and pepper to taste. Cook tomatoes, stirring occasionally, until almost all of their liquid has evaporated, about 15 minutes.

5. Unroll pancetta into long strips and cut into ¾-inch squares. Sauté pancetta in medium-size skillet over medium heat until brown but not crisp, 8 to 10 minutes.

6. Drain potatoes in colander. When cool enough to handle, cut into ¼-inch-thick rounds. Place potatoes in large bowl, sprinkle with vinegar and remaining olive oil, and toss to combine. Add pancetta and fat from pan; toss salad again. Add stewed tomatoes and any oil from pan and salt and pepper to taste. Toss salad once more to combine. Cover bowl with foil and let salad stand 10 to 15 minutes.

7. Place serving dish under hot running water to warm.

8. Dry serving dish. Toss salad to recombine and turn into dish.

Two Pea Soup
Puffy Apple and Onion Omelets
Carrot and Bacon Gratin

The velvety puréed pea soup can precede the apple and onion omelet and baked carrots with their crusty cheese topping.

When preparing the omelets, do not try to save time by making one large omelet with all of the eggs; too many eggs will slow the cooking process, not speed it up. A tender omelet must be cooked quickly.

Presoaking the split peas for the soup cuts the cooking time. This soup, unlike a more traditional version, does not have a smoked meat flavor.

WHAT TO DRINK

A fruity, crisp, dry white wine, such as an Alsatian Riesling or a Pinot Blanc, would be perfect with this menu.

SHOPPING LIST AND STAPLES

2 ounces lean thin-sliced bacon (about 5 slices)
1½ pounds carrots plus 1 small carrot
¾ pound snow peas or sugar snap peas
Small stalk celery
3 medium-size onions
2 tart green apples, preferably Granny Smith or Pippin
8 large eggs
2 ounces Gruyère cheese
½ pint heavy cream
1 stick plus 2 tablespoons unsalted butter

5½ cups chicken stock, preferably homemade
(see page 13), or canned (optional)
1-pound package split peas
½ cup red wine vinegar
Freshly grated nutmeg
Salt and freshly ground pepper

UTENSILS

Blender
Electric mixer
Large heavy-gauge skillet
Small skillet
Omelet pan
2 medium-size saucepans, one with cover
9- or 10-inch gratin dish or shallow flameproof baking dish
3 medium-size bowls
Colander
Strainer
Measuring cups and spoons
Chef's knife
Paring knife
Wooden spoon
Slotted spoon
Metal spatula
Cheese grater
Nutmeg grater
Vegetable peeler

START-TO-FINISH STEPS

The night before or at least 2 hours ahead: Follow soup recipe step 1.

1. Peel onions and thinly slice enough to measure 2½ cups; chop enough onions to measure ½ cup. Peel carrots; set aside 1 small carrot and cut remaining ones diagonally into ½-inch-thick ovals to measure 2 cups.
2. Follow soup recipe steps 2 and 3.
3. Follow omelets recipe steps 1 and 2, and gratin recipe step 1.
4. Follow omelets recipe steps 3 and 4.
5. Follow gratin recipe steps 2 through 6.
6. Follow soup recipe steps 4 and 5.
7. Follow gratin recipe step 7, soup recipe step 6, and serve soup while gratin is baking.
8. Follow gratin recipe steps 8 and 9.
9. Follow omelets recipe steps 5 through 10 and serve with gratin.

RECIPES

Two Pea Soup

1 cup split peas
5½ cups chicken stock or water
Small stalk celery
Small carrot, peeled
½ cup chopped onion

Salt
Freshly ground pepper
¾ pound snow peas or sugar snap peas
¼ cup heavy cream

1. Wash split peas and drain. Combine with 5½ cups water or chicken stock in large saucepan and bring to a boil over medium heat. Boil 2 minutes, remove from heat, and cover pan. Let peas stand in cooking liquid until ready to use.
2. Transfer split peas and their soaking liquid to medium-size pan over medium heat. Rinse and trim celery. Add celery, carrot, onion, and salt and pepper to taste, and stir to combine.
3. Meanwhile, wash snow peas and drain in colander. As soon as split pea liquid reaches a boil, float snow peas on top. Partially cover pan and cook soup at a slow boil until split peas are tender, about 45 minutes.
4. Remove soup from heat. With slotted spoon, remove snow peas, celery, and carrot from pan, and discard. In two batches, transfer soup to blender and purée.
5. Return soup to saucepan, stir in heavy cream, and add salt and pepper to taste.
6. Just before serving, reheat soup over medium heat, stirring frequently. Divide among 4 individual soup bowls.

Puffy Apple and Onion Omelets

5 tablespoons unsalted butter, plus 3 tablespoons chilled
2½ cups thinly sliced onions
2 tart green apples, preferably Granny Smith or Pippin
8 large eggs
3 tablespoons heavy cream
Salt and freshly ground pepper
½ cup red wine vinegar

1. In large heavy-gauge skillet, melt 2 tablespoons butter over medium-low heat. Add onions and stir to coat. Cover and cook 10 minutes, until onions are translucent.
2. Meanwhile, rinse apples and dry. Halve and core apples; slice each half into five ¾-inch crescents.
3. Transfer onions to a plate and set aside. Wipe out skillet with paper towels. Melt 1 tablespoon butter in skillet, add apple slices, and sauté over medium heat until brown, about 1 minute. Turn and brown apples on other side. Do not let apples become too soft.
4. Remove skillet from heat. Add onions and stir to combine; set aside.
5. Break 6 eggs into medium-size bowl. Separate 2 remaining eggs, placing whites in another medium-size bowl and adding yolks to whole eggs. Add heavy cream and salt and pepper to taste to whole eggs and yolks. Beat lightly with fork; set aside.
6. With electric mixer, beat whites at high speed until stiff but not dry, about 2 minutes. Whisk egg and cream mixture to recombine, then fold in whites, incorporating thoroughly.
7. In omelet pan, melt 1 tablespoon butter over medium heat. When butter foams, pour in half of egg mixture. As omelet begins to set, pull edges gently toward center of

pan with fork, allowing uncooked egg to run onto surface of pan. Cook until omelet is brown on bottom but still creamy on surface, 4 to 5 minutes.

8. Spread half of apple-onion filling evenly over one half of omelet; fold free half over to enclose filling. Divide between 2 dinner plates and place in 200-degree oven to keep warm. Repeat process with remaining eggs.

9. When second omelet is done, pour red wine vinegar into skillet used for apple filling, bring to a boil over high heat, and reduce until slightly syrupy. Add chilled butter 1 tablespoon at a time, gently swirling mixture in pan after each addition until butter is incorporated.

10. Remove plates from oven, top each serving with butter-vinegar glaze, and serve.

Carrot and Bacon Gratin

2 ounces lean thin-sliced bacon (about 5 slices)
Salt
2 ounces Gruyère cheese
2 cups sliced carrots
2 tablespoons unsalted butter
¼ cup heavy cream
Freshly grated nutmeg
Freshly ground pepper

1. Dice enough bacon to measure about ⅔ cup and fry in small skillet over medium heat until brown but not crisp. Pour off fat and drain bacon on paper towels.

2. Preheat oven to 425 degrees.

3. In medium-size saucepan, bring 2 quarts water plus 2 tablespoons salt to a boil.

4. Meanwhile, grate enough Gruyère to measure about ½ cup. Cut butter into small pieces.

5. Blanch carrots in boiling water 2 minutes. Turn them into colander, refresh under cold water, and drain.

6. Combine butter, heavy cream, 2 tablespoons grated Gruyère, and a pinch of grated nutmeg in 9- or 10-inch gratin dish or shallow flameproof baking dish. Add carrots, salt and pepper to taste, and toss to combine.

7. Place carrots in oven and bake until cream has thickened and coated carrots, about 20 minutes.

8. Remove carrots from oven. Increase oven temperature to broil. Stir bacon into carrots and sprinkle with remainder of Gruyère. Broil carrots 4 inches from heat until cheese melts and begins to brown, about 2 minutes.

9. Remove gratin from broiler and cover with foil. Reduce oven temperature to 200 degrees and leave oven door ajar for a minute or two to lower temperature more rapidly. Place gratin in oven until ready to serve.

ADDED TOUCH

The chestnuts for this rich dessert are most easily purchased in the winter. Choose glossy, unblemished nuts that seem heavy for their size. One cup of canned, sweetened chestnut purée (or *crème de marrons*) can replace the chestnut cream in this recipe, but reduce the sugar to ⅓ cup in the *crème anglaise*.

Chestnut Ice Cream

The chestnut cream:
30 chestnuts (about 1 pound total weight)
1½ cups milk
¼ cup sugar

The crème anglaise:
1 cup milk
1 cup heavy cream
½ vanilla bean
4 egg yolks
½ cup sugar
1 tablespoon Cognac or rum or kirsch

The chocolate topping (optional)
4 ounces semisweet chocolate
¼ cup plus 2 tablespoons milk

1. Preheat oven to 425 degrees.

2. With paring knife, score each chestnut shell almost completely around circumference. Arrange chestnuts in single layer on 15 x 10-inch baking sheet; sprinkle with 3 or 4 tablespoons water. Roast chestnuts in oven 8 minutes.

3. Using dish towel to protect your hands, peel off outer shells and inner husks of chestnuts while still hot.

4. Combine peeled chestnuts with milk and sugar in medium-size saucepan and bring to a simmer over medium heat. Simmer chestnuts, adding more milk if necessary, until tender, 40 to 60 minutes.

5. Using food processor fitted with steel blade or blender, purée chestnuts with their cooking liquid. Turn purée into medium-size bowl, cover with plastic wrap, and refrigerate 30 minutes.

6. Combine milk and cream with ½ vanilla bean in small heavy-gauge saucepan and set over low heat until mixture is hot but not boiling.

7. In small bowl, combine egg yolks and sugar, and whisk until blended. Add yolk mixture to warm cream mixture and cook, whisking constantly to prevent boiling, until thick enough to coat a spoon, about 5 minutes.

8. Remove pan from heat. Extract vanilla bean, split it lengthwise with paring knife, and scrape out seeds. Add seeds to cream and set aside, stirring occasionally, until cool.

9. When both cream mixtures are completely cooled, fold crème anglaise into chestnut purée. Stir in Cognac. Turn mixture into container of ice-cream maker and freeze according to manufacturer's directions. Or, place mixture in ice-cube trays until partially frozen. Scrape into medium-size bowl and beat with spoon until smooth. Return to ice-cube trays and place in freezer again until partially frozen. Remove partially iced cream and beat as before. Repeat procedure one more time, then return to freezer until frozen through, at least 2 hours.

10. In small saucepan, melt chocolate and milk over very low heat, stirring until blended. When well combined, remove mixture from heat and allow to cool.

11. Divide chestnut ice cream among individual dishes and top each with a spoonful of chocolate sauce.

Howard Helmer and Arlene Wanderman

Although Howard Helmer and Arlene Wanderman are partners, they approach cooking differently. He believes that the time and money spent on a meal should be proportional to the result and that simplicity is important. She believes that no amount of money or time should be spared to produce a dazzling meal.

Over the years they have learned to compromise, creating meals that are easy yet elegant, as these three menus show. The simple chicken-gorgonzola quiche in Menu 1, served with a spicy tomato drink, is perfect for brunch or a light supper. In Menu 2, they create an unusual soufflé with spinach, smoked salmon, two cheeses, and capers, accompanied by a pear and lettuce salad. For dessert, strawberries are flavored with amaretto liqueur and coated with raspberry jam.

Howard Helmer maintains that anything you would put into a sandwich can also go into an omelet. Thus, the Reuben omelets in Menu 3, like the sandwiches after which they are named, contain corned beef, Swiss cheese, and sauerkraut. This quick meal also features a German-style sauté of apple, onion, and potato, and a salad of marinated cucumbers with fresh dill.

This quiche has a country appeal with its wagon-wheel pattern of asparagus spears and cherry tomato halves. The chilled tomato cocktail, garnished with leafy celery stalks, can either precede or accompany the meal.

Spicy Tomato Cocktail
Chicken-Gorgonzola Quiche

To introduce this appetizing meal, offer your guests the tomato cocktail laced with vodka. For a spicier drink, add more horseradish and hot pepper sauce. In cold weather, omit the celery and serve the drink hot in sturdy mugs topped with sour cream.

A quiche is an excellent way to use a variety of ingredients, especially leftover cheeses, meats, poultry, and vegetables. In this quiche, the cooks combine Gorgonzola, Gruyère, and precooked chicken with eggs for the filling, and asparagus spears and cherry tomatoes for the topping. To keep asparagus fresh for several days, stand the stalks upright in a container of water in the refrigerator.

WHAT TO DRINK

Either a light fruity red Beaujolais or a firm white Mâcon-Villages would complement this meal.

SHOPPING LIST AND STAPLES

1 skinless, boneless chicken breast (about 6 ounces)
6 asparagus spears (about ½ pound total weight),
    or 1 small head broccoli
Small bunch celery, with leaves
1 pint cherry tomatoes (optional)
Small bunch scallions
Large lemon
5 large eggs
1 pint half-and-half
1 tablespoon plus 1 teaspoon unsalted butter
¼ pound Gorgonzola cheese
2 ounces Gruyère cheese
12-ounce can tomato juice
⅔ cup chicken stock, preferably homemade (see
    page 13), or canned (optional)
10½-ounce can beef stock
6-ounce package herb-seasoned stuffing mix
4-ounce bottle prepared white horseradish
Worcestershire sauce
Hot pepper sauce
Sugar
Dash of Cayenne pepper
Pinch of freshly grated or ground nutmeg
Salt
Freshly ground pepper
¾ cup vodka

UTENSILS

Small skillet
Medium-size saucepan with cover
10-inch quiche dish or fluted pie pan
Cookie sheet
Large bowl
Medium-size bowl
Small bowl
Measuring cups and spoons
Chef's knife
Paring knife
Wooden spoon
Pie server or metal spatula
Medium-size pitcher
Grater
Juicer
Whisk
Tongs

START-TO-FINISH STEPS

Three hours ahead: For cocktail, place 4 glasses, tomato juice, and beef stock in refrigerator to chill.

1. Follow quiche recipe steps 1 through 7.
2. Follow cocktail recipe steps 1 and 2.
3. Follow quiche recipe steps 8 through 11.
4. Follow cocktail recipe step 3, quiche recipe step 12, and serve.

RECIPES

Spicy Tomato Cocktail

Large lemon
4 stalks celery, with leaves
12-ounce can tomato juice
10½-ounce can beef stock
¾ cup vodka
2 tablespoons prepared white horseradish
1 teaspoon Worcestershire sauce
¼ teaspoon hot pepper sauce
Freshly ground pepper

1. Squeeze lemon and set juice aside. Rinse celery stalks, dry with paper towels, trim ends, and refrigerate until needed.
2. Combine lemon and tomato juices, beef stock, and

48

vodka in medium-size pitcher; stir gently. Add horse-radish, Worcestershire and hot pepper sauces, and freshly ground pepper to taste; stir to blend. Place pitcher in coldest part of refrigerator until needed.

3. Just before serving, stir cocktail thoroughly to recombine. Pour cocktail into chilled glasses and garnish with celery stalks.

Chicken-Gorgonzola Quiche

1 skinless, boneless chicken breast (about 6 ounces)
Salt and freshly ground pepper
1 tablespoon plus 1 teaspoon unsalted butter
4 scallions
3 cups herb-seasoned stuffing mix
⅔ cup chicken stock
5 large eggs
¼ pound Gorgonzola cheese
2 ounces Gruyère cheese
1 cup half-and-half
Pinch of sugar
Pinch of freshly grated or ground nutmeg
Dash of Cayenne pepper
6 asparagus spears (about ½ pound total weight), or
   1 small head broccoli
6 cherry tomatoes (optional)

1. Rinse chicken breast and dry with paper towels. Season with salt and pepper to taste. In small skillet, melt 1 tablespoon butter over medium-high heat. Sauté chicken 3 to 4 minutes on each side until lightly browned. Transfer chicken to plate until cool enough to handle; then dice enough to measure 1 cup. Cover and set aside.

2. Preheat oven to 375 degrees.

3. Rinse scallions and dry with paper towels. Trim scallions and slice thinly to measure about ½ cup. Melt remaining teaspoon butter in small skillet over medium heat. Sauté scallions, stirring occasionally, until white parts are soft, about 3 minutes. Remove from heat.

4. In large bowl, combine stuffing mix with chicken stock until well blended. Lightly beat 1 egg in small bowl. Add egg to stuffing mix and stir to combine.

5. Press stuffing into quiche dish, lining bottom and sides; crimp edges. Place on cookie sheet in oven and bake 5 minutes.

6. While shell is baking, crumble Gorgonzola to measure ½ cup, and set aside. Grate Gruyère to measure ½ cup and set aside. Beat remaining 4 eggs in medium-size bowl until blended. Beat in half-and-half, chicken, Gorgonzola, Gruyère, sugar, nutmeg, Cayenne pepper, and salt and pepper to taste.

7. Remove shell from oven and pour in half of chicken-cheese mixture; place quiche on cookie sheet in oven and carefully pour in remainder of mixture. Bake 35 to 40 minutes.

8. Bring 2 inches of water to a boil in medium-size saucepan. Using paring knife, trim off woody ends of asparagus spears. Peel stalks (see following illustration), if desired, and cut into 5-inch lengths; rinse under cold water.

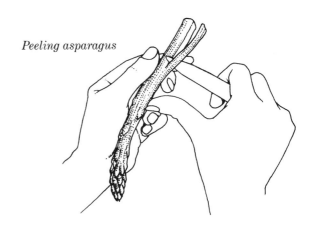
Peeling asparagus

9. Add 1 teaspoon salt to boiling water; then add asparagus. Simmer, covered, just until crisp-tender, 4 to 10 minutes depending on size of asparagus. With tongs, remove asparagus to plate lined with paper towels.

10. Carefully pull out oven rack and arrange asparagus spears in wheel-spoke pattern on top of partially baked quiche. Continue baking quiche until tip of knife inserted in center comes out clean, about 5 minutes.

11. If using cherry tomatoes for garnish, rinse, dry, and cut in half.

12. Remove quiche from oven and garnish with cherry tomato halves, if desired.

ADDED TOUCH

Amaretto (a sweet liqueur) and amarettini (tiny, crunchy macaroon cookies) add an almond flavor to these baked pears.

Baked Stuffed Pears

15 amarettini or 5 amaretto cookies
½ cup walnuts
1 teaspoon plus 2 teaspoons unsalted butter
2 teaspoons amaretto liqueur
2 teaspoons rum
4 medium-size firm pears, such as Anjou, Comice,
   or Forelle
1 quart vanilla ice cream (optional)

1. Preheat oven to 350 degrees.

2. In food processor fitted with steel blade or in blender, crush amarettini. Add nuts and pulse just to chop. Add 1 teaspoon butter and 1 teaspoon each amaretto and rum; pulse once to blend.

3. Rinse pears and dry with paper towels. Peel, halve, and core pears; arrange in baking dish, cut side up.

4. Using teaspoon, mound amarettini filling in pear halves. Dot with remaining 2 teaspoons butter and drizzle with remaining teaspoons amaretto and rum. Pour hot water to depth of about ¼ inch in baking dish.

5. Bake pears 20 minutes, or until golden brown. Remove from oven and, with slotted spoon, arrange 2 pear halves on each dessert plate. Serve with vanilla ice cream, if desired.

Spinach and Smoked Salmon Soufflé
Bibb Lettuce and Pears in Walnut Vinaigrette
Amaretto Strawberries Melba

For an elegant buffet, set out the salad and dessert, fill the wine glasses, then bring out the soufflé at the last minute.

Capers and smoked salmon lend their distinctive flavors to this soufflé. Capers—the unopened flower buds of a wild shrub common to the Mediterranean—are often packed in vinegar, in which case be sure to rinse them before using. Smoked salmon is cured with salt and then lightly smoked. Because it is extremely perishable, refrigerate the salmon sealed tightly in foil or plastic wrap and use it within a week.

WHAT TO DRINK

A dry white wine with good body such as a California Chardonnay will go well with this dinner.

SHOPPING LIST AND STAPLES

¼ pound smoked salmon
2 heads Bibb lettuce
Small bunch scallions
2 pints strawberries
Small ripe pear
7 large eggs
1½ cups milk
½ pint sour cream
1 stick plus 4 tablespoons unsalted butter
¼ pound Gruyère cheese
2 ounces Parmesan cheese, approximately
10-ounce package frozen chopped spinach
¼ cup raspberry jam
1 tablespoon capers
¼ cup walnut oil
2 tablespoons white wine vinegar
⅓ cup flour
¾ teaspoon cream of tartar
3-ounce package walnut pieces
Salt and freshly ground pepper
2 tablespoons amaretto liqueur

UTENSILS

Food processor or blender (optional)
Electric mixer
Medium-size heavy-gauge saucepan
2-quart soufflé dish
2 large bowls
2 medium-size bowls
2 small bowls
Colander

Salad spinner (optional)
Large strainer
Measuring cups and spoons
Chef's knife
Paring knife
Wooden spoon
Rubber spatula
Grater
Whisk

START-TO-FINISH STEPS

At least one hour ahead: Remove spinach for soufflé recipe from freezer to defrost.

1. Follow soufflé recipe steps 1 through 11.
2. While soufflé bakes, follow salad recipe steps 1 through 3.
3. Follow strawberries recipe steps 1 through 3.
4. Follow salad recipe step 4.
5. Follow soufflé recipe step 12 and serve with salad. Serve strawberries for dessert.

RECIPES

Spinach and Smoked Salmon Soufflé

10-ounce package frozen chopped spinach, thawed
¼ pound Gruyère cheese
2 ounces Parmesan cheese, approximately
1 stick plus 4 tablespoons unsalted butter
⅓ cup flour
1½ cups milk
3 scallions
¼ pound smoked salmon
1 tablespoon capers
7 large eggs
¾ teaspoon cream of tartar

1. Preheat oven to 350 degrees.
2. Place spinach in strainer over medium-size bowl and squeeze out as much liquid as possible. Set aside.
3. Grate Gruyère to measure about 1 cup and Parmesan to measure about ¼ cup. Set aside separately.
4. Make 4-inch-wide collar of double-thickness aluminum foil for 2-quart soufflé dish. Tie collar around dish, allowing 2-inch band to extend above rim (see illustration on following page). Butter inside of collar and dish; dust lightly with some of the Parmesan.

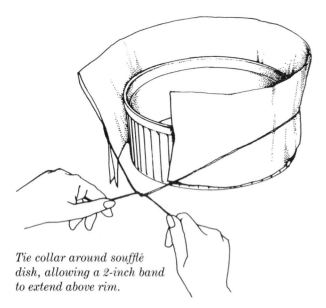

Tie collar around soufflé dish, allowing a 2-inch band to extend above rim.

5. Melt butter in heavy-gauge saucepan over medium-high heat. When butter stops foaming, whisk in flour until blended. Cook mixture, stirring constantly, 2 to 3 minutes, until smooth and bubbly. Add milk all at once and, continuing to stir, cook until sauce comes to a boil and is smooth and thickened, 4 to 5 minutes. Remove from heat.

6. Rinse scallions, dry with paper towels, and trim; chop to measure about ½ cup. Chop salmon and capers finely. Or, if using food processor fitted with steel blade or blender, process scallions, salmon, and capers together just until blended. Mixture should retain a little texture.

7. Add salmon, scallions, and capers to sauce in pan; stir to combine. Add Gruyère, Parmesan, and spinach and stir until well blended.

8. Separate eggs, placing whites in large bowl and 6 yolks in small bowl. Reserve extra yolk for another use. Beat yolks to combine, then pour into saucepan and blend thoroughly with cheese mixture.

9. Using electric mixer, beat egg whites with cream of tartar at high speed, 4 to 5 minutes, or just until stiff peaks form.

10. With rubber spatula, stir approximately ¼ cup beaten egg white into cheese mixture, then fold in remaining whites.

11. Pour mixture into prepared soufflé dish. Bake 30 to 40 minutes, until soufflé is puffed and delicately browned. (Do not open oven door to check on soufflé for at least 20 to 25 minutes.)

12. Remove soufflé from oven. Remove collar from dish and place soufflé on table. Break crust with serving spoon, divide among 4 plates, and top with soufflé.

Bibb Lettuce and Pears in Walnut Vinaigrette

2 heads Bibb lettuce
¼ cup walnut oil
2 tablespoons white wine vinegar
Salt and freshly ground pepper
Small ripe pear
¼ cup walnut pieces

1. Wash lettuce, separate leaves, and dry in salad spinner or with paper towels; wrap in plastic bag and refrigerate.

2. Combine oil, vinegar, and salt and pepper to taste in small bowl. Whisk until blended; set aside.

3. Rinse pear and pat dry; cut into quarters and core. Slice each quarter lengthwise into 3 pieces. Place slices in large bowl, add about 2 tablespoons dressing, and stir gently to coat slices and prevent them from turning brown. Cover bowl with plastic wrap and refrigerate.

4. Just before serving, arrange lettuce leaves on plates and top with pear slices. Whisk dressing to recombine and pour over salad. Sprinkle with chopped nuts.

Amaretto Strawberries Melba

1½ pints strawberries
2 tablespoons amaretto liqueur
¼ cup raspberry jam
¼ cup sour cream

1. Wash, drain, hull, and cut strawberries in half.

2. Place berries in medium-size bowl and sprinkle with amaretto. Add raspberry jam and stir gently with wooden spoon until berries are evenly coated.

3. Divide berries among 4 wine glasses or sherbet cups, reserving 8 halves. Top each serving with a tablespoonful of sour cream and 2 strawberry halves. Refrigerate until ready to serve.

ADDED TOUCH

You can substitute brown rice here, but follow package directions—cooking time and amount of water required differ from wild rice.

Wild Rice Pilaf

½ teaspoon salt
¾ cup wild rice
1 stalk celery
¼ pound mushrooms
Small onion
2 tablespoons unsalted butter
Freshly ground pepper

1. Bring 2¼ cups water and salt to a boil in medium-size saucepan with tight-fitting lid.

2. Rinse rice in large strainer under hot water.

3. Add rice to boiling water, stir, and cover. Return water to a boil, reduce heat, and simmer 35 to 40 minutes.

4. Meanwhile, wash celery, dry with paper towel, trim, and peel; slice thinly to measure about ½ cup. Wipe mushrooms with damp paper towels and slice thinly to measure about 1⅓ cups. Peel onion and chop to measure ¼ cup.

5. Melt butter in large skillet and sauté vegetables over medium-high heat until onion is translucent, about 5 minutes. Set aside.

6. When rice is done, toss with vegetables in skillet and sauté 2 to 3 minutes. Season pilaf with salt and pepper to taste and serve.

Reuben Omelets
Marinated Cucumbers with Dill
Apple, Onion, and Potato Sauté

This German-inspired meal features a hearty Reuben omelet, sautéed apples, onions, and potatoes, and a tart salad.

You might expect a Reuben omelet to be topped with the traditional Russian dressing. However, the cooks use their own version of Thousand Island instead. Their recipe contains chili sauce and sweet gherkins (tiny pickled cucumbers), which when chopped are said to resemble the thousands of tiny islands in the St. Lawrence River.

WHAT TO DRINK

Beer is the best choice for this menu, whether you like it pale, dark, heavy, or light.

SHOPPING LIST AND STAPLES

12 thin slices corned beef (about ¾ pound total weight)
2 medium-size Idaho potatoes (¾ to 1 pound total weight)
2 medium-size tart, green apples, such as Granny Smith
   (¾ to 1 pound total weight)
2 medium-size cucumbers (about 1 pound total weight)
Medium-size onion
Large lemon
Small head red leaf lettuce
Small bunch fresh dill, or 2 teaspoons dried
11 large eggs

5 tablespoons unsalted butter, approximately
8 thin slices Swiss cheese (5 to 6 ounces total weight)
½-pound package sauerkraut
12-ounce jar chili sauce
8-ounce jar whole sweet gherkins
1 cup plus 3 tablespoons safflower oil
1½ tablespoons white wine vinegar
2 teaspoons Dijon mustard
1 tablespoon light brown sugar
1 teaspoon caraway seeds
Pinch of ground allspice
Salt and freshly ground pepper

UTENSILS

Food processor or blender
Large skillet with cover
10-inch nonstick or well-seasoned omelet pan
2 medium-size bowls
2 small bowls
Salad spinner (optional)
Measuring cups and spoons
Large strainer
Chef's knife
Paring knife
Wooden spoon
Vinyl spatula
Juicer
Whisk
Vegetable scrub brush
Scissors

START-TO-FINISH STEPS

One hour ahead: Set out Swiss cheese, corned beef, sauerkraut, eggs, and butter to bring to room temperature for omelets recipe.

1. Coarsely chop 6 gherkins for dressing recipe. If using gherkins to garnish omelets, score each one four times, three quarters through on crosswise slant; set aside.
2. Follow omelets recipe steps 1 and 2.
3. Follow dressing recipe steps 1 through 3.
4. Follow cucumbers recipe steps 1 through 5.
5. Follow potato recipe steps 1 through 5.
6. Follow omelets recipe steps 3 through 7.
7. Follow dressing recipe step 4, omelets recipe step 8, and serve with potato sauté and cucumbers.

RECIPES

Reuben Omelets

1 cup sauerkraut
8 large eggs
1 teaspoon caraway seeds
4 tablespoons unsalted butter
8 thin slices Swiss cheese (5 to 6 ounces total weight)
12 thin slices corned beef (about ¾ pound total weight)
Thousand Island Dressing (see following recipe)
8 whole sweet gherkins, scored, for garnish (optional)

1. Preheat oven to 200 degrees. Place 4 dinner plates in oven to warm.
2. Drain sauerkraut in large strainer.
3. Break eggs into medium-size bowl; add ½ cup water and caraway seeds. Beat until well blended.
4. Place nonstick or well-seasoned omelet pan over medium-high heat until a drop of water sizzles on its surface. Melt 1 tablespoon butter in pan, tilting to coat bottom and sides. Quickly pour one quarter of egg mixture into pan; edges will set immediately. Slip inverted spatula under edge of omelet; slide spatula around pan, pulling cooked edges of omelet toward center and tilting pan so uncooked egg flows onto exposed surface. Omelet should cook in about 40 seconds. The top will be moist and creamy.
5. On one half of omelet, layer 2 slices of Swiss cheese, 3 slices of corned beef, and ¼ cup sauerkraut. Using spatula, fold unfilled side of omelet over filling.
6. Turn omelet onto warmed plate; place in oven to keep warm.
7. Wipe out pan, if necessary, with paper towels. Repeat process for 3 more omelets.
8. When all omelets are cooked, top each with one quarter of Thousand Island Dressing, garnish with 2 scored gherkins, if desired, and serve immediately.

Thousand Island Dressing

Large lemon
3 large eggs
6 whole sweet gherkins, coarsely chopped
⅓ cup chili sauce
2 teaspoons Dijon mustard
1 cup safflower oil

1. Squeeze enough lemon juice to measure 2 tablespoons.
2. Separate 2 eggs, placing yolks in small bowl and reserv-

ing whites for another use. Break remaining whole egg into yolks and beat briefly to combine.

3. Place eggs, lemon juice, gherkins, chili sauce, and mustard in food processor fitted with steel blade or in blender. Process or blend 10 seconds. Then, with appliance running, slowly drizzle oil into mixture. Process or blend until dressing has the consistency of mayonnaise.

4. Just before serving, recombine, if necessary.

Marinated Cucumbers with Dill

Small head red leaf lettuce
Small bunch fresh dill, or 2 teaspoons dried
2 medium-size cucumbers (about 1 pound total weight)
3 tablespoons safflower oil
1½ tablespoons white wine vinegar
Salt
Freshly ground pepper

1. Separate lettuce leaves. Wash, dry in salad spinner or with paper towels, and divide among 4 salad plates.
2. If using fresh dill, rinse and dry; snip enough to measure 2 tablespoons.
3. Peel cucumbers, cut in half lengthwise, and seed. Cut crosswise into ¼-inch-thick slices and place in medium-size bowl.
4. In small bowl, combine oil, vinegar, and salt and freshly ground pepper to taste. Beat mixture until well blended.
5. Pour dressing over cucumbers, add dill, and toss to combine. Arrange cucumbers on lettuce; refrigerate until ready to serve.

Apple, Onion, and Potato Sauté

2 medium-size Idaho potatoes (¾ to 1 pound total weight)
1 tablespoon unsalted butter, approximately
Medium-size onion
2 medium-size tart green apples, such as Granny Smith (¾ to 1 pound total weight)
1 tablespoon light brown sugar
Pinch of ground allspice
Salt
Freshly ground pepper

1. Wash and scrub potatoes, but do not peel. Dry with paper towels, then cut into ⅛-inch-thick rounds.
2. Melt butter in large skillet, add potatoes, and sauté over medium heat 8 to 12 minutes.
3. While potatoes are cooking, peel and thinly slice onion.

Rinse apples and pat dry, but do not peel. Core and cut apples in half lengthwise. With cut side down, slice each half into ¼-inch-thick slices.

4. Add apples, onion, and more butter, if necessary, to skillet. Stir mixture to combine; sauté 7 minutes, or until potatoes and apples are just barely tender. Do not overcook.
5. Add brown sugar, allspice, and salt and pepper to taste; stir to combine. Turn off heat and cover skillet.

ADDED TOUCH

Streusel—German for "sprinkling"—is a crunchy topping often used on coffee cakes. It is perfect here for baked oranges.

Oranges with Pecan Streusel

4 tablespoons plus 1 tablespoon unsalted butter, softened
4 large navel oranges
1 to 2 tablespoons orange liqueur, such as Cointreau or Grand Marnier
1 egg
⅔ cup lightly packed light brown sugar
½ cup flour
½ cup chopped pecans
1 teaspoon ground cinnamon
½ pint heavy cream for garnish (optional)

1. Preheat oven to 375 degrees. Butter 11 x 7-inch baking dish.
2. Peel oranges, removing as much white pith as possible. Cut off ends of each orange and slice in half crosswise. Arrange slices in baking dish and sprinkle with orange liqueur.
3. Separate egg, placing yolk in medium-size bowl; reserve white for another use. Beat yolk lightly.
4. Add brown sugar, flour, pecans, cinnamon, and 4 tablespoons butter to egg yolk. Work mixture with fingers just until combined and crumbly.
5. Spoon 2 to 3 tablespoons of crumb mixture on top of each orange slice and dot with remaining tablespoon butter. Bake oranges 25 minutes, or until streusel topping is golden brown.
6. If using for garnish, whip cream with electric mixer in chilled medium-size bowl until it stands in stiff peaks. Refrigerate until needed.
7. Serve dessert warm or at room temperature, topped with whipped cream, if desired.

Penelope Casas

MENU 1 (Right)
Eggs in Nests
Piparrada Salad
Spinach with Raisins and Pine Nuts

MENU 2
Pan-Set Eggs with Lima Beans and Artichokes
Catalan Garlic Bread
Salad Madrileño

MENU 3
Spanish-Style Soft-Set Eggs
Sauté of Red Bell Peppers
Watercress, Carrot, and Endive Salad
in Anchovy Vinaigrette

Spanish cooking varies from region to region, but eggs are used throughout the country. According to Penelope Casas, who made her first visit to Spain over twenty years ago, "It is hard to imagine a Spanish meal that does not include eggs in several guises." All three of her menus feature Spanish-style eggs as the main course.

For Menu 1, she offers eggs in nests—hollowed-out rolls—a recipe handed down to her by her Spanish mother-in-law. A seasoned tomato sauce forms the bottom layer in the roll, an egg yolk the middle layer, and a crown of beaten egg whites the top. Two other Spanish dishes accompany the eggs: a salad version of *piparrada* (a Basque specialty combining peppers, onions, and tomatoes) and spinach with raisins and pine nuts.

The eggs in Menu 2 cook in covered skillets with lima beans and artichoke hearts and are served with a kind of garlic bread popular in Catalonia in northeastern Spain. The soft-set eggs in Menu 3 are similar to scrambled eggs, but are prepared in a double boiler fashioned from two skillets to give them a more delicate consistency. This meal also includes sautéed red pepper strips and a watercress, carrot, and endive salad dressed with an anchovy-flavored vinaigrette.

Set a bright fiesta table with flowers and colorful pottery to go with the Spanish-style ham-and-egg-filled rolls and piparrada salad. The lightly cooked spinach is mixed with golden raisins and subtly sweet pine nuts.

Eggs in Nests
Piparrada Salad
Spinach with Raisins and Pine Nuts

For the nests, you can use egg twist rolls, bow knot rolls, or any roll with a firm crust that will not become soggy when filled and baked. Store pine nuts *(pignoli)* in a jar in the refrigerator because they spoil quickly.

WHAT TO DRINK

Try a white Rioja with this menu or use it to make a wine punch. Mix 1 bottle of Rioja, 2 tablespoons of orange juice, and 1 tablespoon of sugar with orange and lemon slices. Chill until ready to serve, then stir in 1 cup of club soda.

SHOPPING LIST AND STAPLES

¼ pound cured ham, such as prosciutto
1½ pounds spinach
2 medium-size tomatoes (about 1 pound total weight)
Medium-size cucumber
Large green bell pepper
Small onion
Large shallot
Small bunch scallions
2 cloves garlic, 1 large and 1 small
Small bunch parsley
8 small eggs
6-ounce can tomato paste
4-ounce jar whole pimientos (optional)
½ cup olive oil, approximately
¼ cup plus 2 tablespoons vegetable oil
3 tablespoons white wine vinegar
8 medium-size rolls, such as egg twist or bow knot
3 tablespoons golden raisins
2-ounce jar pine nuts
Pinch of dried thyme
Salt and freshly ground pepper

UTENSILS

Electric mixer
Medium-size skillet
Large saucepan with cover
Small saucepan
15 x 10-inch baking sheet
Large bowl
Medium-size bowl
Small bowl
Colander
Measuring cups and spoons

Chef's knife
Paring knife
Wooden spoon
Metal spatula
Pastry brush
Whisk
Vegetable peeler (optional)

START-TO-FINISH STEPS

1. Peel garlic cloves: Mince large clove to measure 1 tablespoon for spinach recipe; mince small clove to measure 1 teaspoon for salad recipe. Rinse parsley and dry with paper towels; chop enough to measure 2 tablespoons for eggs recipe, for spinach recipe, and 1 tablespoon, if using, for salad recipe.
2. Follow salad recipe steps 1 through 3.
3. Follow eggs recipe steps 1 through 4.
4. While sauce cooks, follow spinach recipe steps 1 through 3 and eggs recipe step 5.
5. Follow spinach recipe steps 4 and 5, and eggs recipe steps 6 through 8.
6. Follow salad recipe step 4, eggs recipe step 9, and serve with spinach.

RECIPES

Eggs in Nests

Small bunch scallions
¼ cup, approximately, plus 2 tablespoons olive oil
¼ pound cured ham, such as prosciutto
¼ cup plus 2 tablespoons tomato paste
Salt and freshly ground pepper
8 medium-size rolls, such as egg twist or bow knot
8 small eggs
2 tablespoons chopped parsley

1. Preheat oven to 450 degrees.
2. Rinse scallions, dry with paper towels, and chop enough white part to measure ¼ cup. Reserve remainder of scallions for another use. Heat 2 tablespoons olive oil in small saucepan over medium heat. Add scallions and cook, stirring frequently, until soft, about 5 minutes.
3. Dice ham, add to pan, and sauté 2 to 3 minutes, or just until scallions are lightly browned.
4. Stir in tomato paste, ¾ cup water, and salt and pepper to taste. Bring mixture to a simmer and cook, stirring

occasionally, about 20 minutes. If mixture becomes too thick, add enough water to obtain desired consistency.

5. Cut a 1½-inch circular plug from middle of each roll, keeping bottom intact. Hollow out rolls, leaving bottoms about 1¼-inches thick and sides ½-inch thick. Discard bread from hollows or reserve for another use. Place hollow rolls on 15 x 10-inch baking sheet. Spoon about 1½ tablespoons of sauce into each roll.

6. Separate eggs, catching whites in large bowl and carefully slipping yolks into hollow rolls. Brush outsides of rolls with remaining olive oil.

7. Using an electric mixer, beat egg whites with a pinch of salt at high speed until stiff but not dry. Spoon egg white into hollow of each roll, making 2-inch-high dome. Reserve leftover egg white for another use.

8. Place nests in oven and bake 5 minutes, or until egg whites are lightly golden.

9. With spatula, transfer 2 nests to each dinner plate, garnish with parsley, and serve.

Piparrada Salad

Large green bell pepper
Medium-size cucumber
Small onion
1 whole pimiento (optional)
2 medium-size tomatoes (about 1 pound total weight)
¼ cup plus 2 tablespoons vegetable oil
3 tablespoons white wine vinegar
1 teaspoon minced garlic
Salt and freshly ground pepper
1 tablespoon chopped parsley (optional)

1. Rinse, core, halve, and seed bell pepper. Remove membranes and cut pepper into 1-inch-wide strips (see illustration below); cut strips in half crosswise. Peel cucumber, cut in half lengthwise; then cut halves crosswise into ½-inch-thick slices. Peel onion and chop enough to measure ¼ cup. If using pimiento, drain, and cut into julienne strips. Rinse tomatoes, dry with paper towels, and cut in half; cut halves into ½-inch-thick slices.

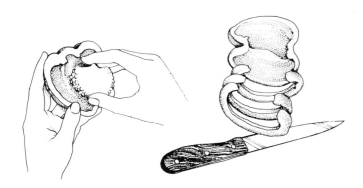

2. Whisk oil and vinegar together in medium-size bowl. Whisk in garlic and salt and pepper to taste.

3. Stir in bell pepper, cucumber, onion and tomatoes until coated with dressing. Cover bowl with plastic wrap and refrigerate until ready to serve.

4. Toss salad, divide among individual plates, and garnish with parsley and pimiento, if desired.

Spinach with Raisins and Pine Nuts

1½ pounds spinach
3 tablespoons golden raisins
Large shallot
Salt
2 tablespoons olive oil
1 tablespoon minced garlic
1 tablespoon chopped parsley
Pinch of dried thyme
3 tablespoons pine nuts
Freshly ground pepper

1. Remove and discard spinach stems. Wash leaves well and drain in colander; do not dry.

2. Place raisins in small bowl with enough warm water to cover. Peel and mince shallot to measure 2 tablespoons.

3. Place spinach in large saucepan and sprinkle lightly with salt. Cook spinach, covered, over medium-high heat about 5 minutes, or until wilted. Turn spinach into colander to drain.

4. Heat olive oil in medium-size skillet. Add shallots and garlic, and sauté about 5 minutes over medium heat until shallots are soft.

5. Drain raisins and add to skillet along with spinach, parsley, and thyme. Stir in pine nuts, salt and pepper to taste, and cook, stirring occasionally, until flavors are combined and spinach heated through, about 5 minutes.

ADDED TOUCH

This easy fruit and wine compote is a traditional Basque dessert. It will keep for weeks in a jar in the refrigerator, but warm it before serving to bring out the subtle flavors.

Dried Fruit Compote

1 lemon
1 orange
¾ cup red wine
¼ cup cream sherry
¼ to ½ cup packed light brown sugar
¼ cup honey
1 stick cinnamon
4 cups mixed dried fruits, such as pitted prunes, apricots, peaches, or apples (about 1 pound total weight)

1. Rinse lemon and orange and cut each in half; peel one half of each, removing as much white pith as possible; slice peels finely.

2. Combine lemon and orange peels with remaining ingredients and 1 cup water in medium-size saucepan. Bring mixture to a boil, reduce heat, and simmer, covered, 15 minutes, or until fruits are soft. Remove cinnamon stick; set compote aside in pan, covered.

3. When ready to serve, warm compote briefly over low heat. Immediately spoon fruit into large serving bowl or divide among individual dessert dishes.

Pan-Set Eggs with Lima Beans and Artichokes
Catalan Garlic Bread
Salad Madrileño

Eggs with lima beans and artichokes, garlic-tomato bread, and salad make a quick meal for unexpected guests.

oth saffron and ground cumin season the pan-set eggs. Although cumin is widely available pre-ground, it is best freshly ground. Lightly roast ¼ cup of cumin seeds in an ungreased skillet to intensify their flavor, stirring constantly over medium heat. When they have turned a light chocolate color, remove them from the pan and cool. Crush the seeds between two sheets of waxed paper with a rolling pin.

For the garlic bread, select a firm-textured Italian- or French-style loaf that will hold up when you rub it with the ripe tomato.

WHAT TO DRINK

Enjoy this Spanish meal with a good Spanish wine, such as a full-bodied red Rioja.

SHOPPING LIST AND STAPLES

3½-ounce can light-meat tuna
Small head Romaine lettuce
4 medium-size very ripe tomatoes
1¼ pounds lima beans or two 10-ounce packages frozen
Small white onion
Small red onion
6 to 7 medium-size cloves garlic
Medium-size bunch parsley
8 large eggs
10-ounce package frozen artichoke hearts
1-pound jar white asparagus (optional)
½ cup chicken stock, preferably homemade (see page 13), or canned
4¾-ounce jar small green Spanish olives, preferably without pimiento
½ cup plus 3 tablespoons olive oil
¼ cup plus 2 tablespoons white wine vinegar
1 teaspoon Dijon mustard
1 loaf Italian or French bread, preferably round
Pinch of sugar
Large pinch of saffron threads
1 teaspoon ground cumin
2 bay leaves
Salt and freshly ground pepper

UTENSILS

2 large skillets with covers
Baking sheet
2 small bowls
Salad spinner (optional)
Measuring cups and spoons
Chef's knife
Paring knife
Wooden spoon
Wide metal spatula
Small whisk
Pastry brush

START-TO-FINISH STEPS

One hour ahead: For eggs recipe, set out frozen artichoke hearts and lima beans, if using, to thaw. Set out eggs to bring to room temperature.

1. Prepare tomatoes, onions, and garlic.
2. Follow salad recipe steps 1 through 3.
3. Follow eggs recipe steps 1 through 4.
4. While vegetables cook, follow bread recipe steps 1 through 3.
5. Follow eggs recipe step 5 and bread recipe step 4.
6. Follow eggs recipe step 6, bread recipe step 5, and salad recipe step 4.

RECIPES

Pan-Set Eggs with Lima Beans and Artichokes

2 tablespoons olive oil
3 tablespoons chopped white onion
1½ tablespoons minced garlic
½ cup very ripe chopped tomato
Medium-size bunch parsley
8 frozen artichoke hearts, thawed
3 cups lima beans
½ cup chicken stock
2 bay leaves
Large pinch of saffron threads
1 teaspoon ground cumin
Salt and freshly ground pepper
8 large eggs

1. Place 1 tablespoon olive oil in each of 2 large skillets over medium heat. Divide onion and garlic between skillets and sauté until onion is translucent, about 5 minutes.
2. Add ¼ cup chopped tomato to each skillet and cook, stirring occasionally, until sauce is slightly thickened, about 3 minutes.

61

3. Wash parsley, dry with paper towels, and mince enough to measure 5 tablespoons. Halve artichoke hearts.
4. Divide the following ingredients, adding half to each skillet: artichokes, lima beans, chicken stock, bay leaves, saffron threads, and cumin. Add salt and pepper to taste to each skillet. Divide 3 tablespoons parsley between skillets. Stir mixtures to combine, add about 5 tablespoons water to each skillet, cover both, and cook vegetables over medium-low heat until almost tender, about 10 minutes.
5. One at a time, break eggs, and drop, 4 per skillet, on top of vegetable mixture, spacing evenly. Cover skillets tightly and continue cooking over medium-low heat until whites are just set and yolks are still soft, about 5 minutes.
6. With wide spatula, divide eggs with vegetables among dinner plates and sprinkle with remaining parsley.

Catalan Garlic Bread

1 loaf Italian or French bread, preferably round
¼ cup plus 2 tablespoons olive oil
4 teaspoons minced garlic
Medium-size very ripe tomato, halved

1. Preheat oven to 350 degrees.
2. From center of loaf, cut four ¾-inch-thick slices of bread. Lay bread on baking sheet and toast in oven, turning once, until lightly browned on both sides, about 10 minutes.
3. While bread toasts, combine olive oil and garlic in small bowl, stirring with fork.
4. Remove toasted bread from oven, leaving heat on. Rub both sides of bread slices with cut side of tomato; discard tomato. Using pastry brush, lightly spread olive oil-garlic mixture on toast.
5. Place toast on baking sheet and return to oven just to crisp, 3 to 4 minutes. Serve warm with eggs.

Salad Madrileño

Small head Romaine lettuce
4 white asparagus spears (optional)
2 medium-size very ripe tomatoes, cut in wedges
4 thin slices red onion
3½-ounce can light-meat tuna
16 small green Spanish olives, preferably without pimiento
3 tablespoons olive oil
¼ cup plus 2 tablespoons white wine vinegar
1 teaspoon Dijon mustard

Pinch of sugar
Salt
Freshly ground pepper

1. Separate lettuce into leaves, wash, and dry in salad spinner or with paper towels. Tear enough leaves to measure about 6 cups and divide lettuce among 4 salad plates. If using asparagus spears, cut off ends.
2. Arrange 2 tomato wedges, 1 slice onion, one quarter of tuna, 1 asparagus spear, and 4 olives on top of lettuce on each plate. Cover plates with plastic wrap and refrigerate.
3. Combine olive oil, vinegar, mustard, sugar, and salt and pepper to taste in small bowl and whisk well to combine. Set aside until ready to serve.
4. Just before serving, stir dressing to recombine and spoon over salad.

Drambuie is a liqueur made from fine Scotch whiskey, herbs, and heather honey. Kirsch, or *kirschwasser*, is a clear cherry brandy. You may substitute any fruit liqueur for either one.

Strawberry "Soup" with Vanilla Ice Cream

3 pints fresh strawberries, or 6 cups whole frozen strawberries, thawed
Medium-size orange
¼ cup dry sherry
¼ cup kirsch
¼ cup Drambuie
2 sticks cinnamon
¼ cup sugar
Pinch of salt
1 pint vanilla ice cream

1. If using fresh strawberries, wash, hull, and coarsely chop enough to measure 6 cups. If using frozen, chop thawed berries. Halve orange and squeeze enough juice to measure ¼ cup.
2. Combine strawberries, orange juice, sherry, kirsch, Drambuie, cinnamon sticks, sugar, and salt in large saucepan. Bring liquid to a boil over medium-high heat, reduce to a simmer, and cook, uncovered, about 10 minutes, or until strawberries are soft.
3. Remove pan from heat and cover to keep warm. When ready to serve, divide strawberry mixture among 4 dessert bowls and top with a scoop of ice cream.

Spanish-Style Soft-Set Eggs
Sauté of Red Bell Peppers
Watercress, Carrot, and Endive Salad in Anchovy Vinaigrette

For a late-night supper or weekend brunch, serve soft-set eggs combined with crabmeat and prosciutto and red bell peppers sautéed with garlic. A salad of watercress, carrot, and endive is the colorful side dish.

Prosciutto, a dry-cured ham, is deep pink, moist, and only mildly salty; it is the best choice for this egg recipe. Commonly sold in Italian markets and some specialty food shops, prosciutto is also packaged presliced. You can substitute a cured or boiled ham—but not a smoked one.

If fresh crab is unavailable at your fish dealer, use either the canned variety that is labeled "fresh" or frozen crabmeat. Remove all bits of cartilage and shell before cooking.

WHAT TO DRINK

The cook suggests a dry white wine from the Penedes region of Catalonia. If unavailable, look for a white Rioja.

SHOPPING LIST AND STAPLES

¼ pound medium-size shrimp, or 8-ounce package frozen
2 ounces fresh crabmeat (about ⅓ cup), or 6-ounce package frozen, or 1-pound can pasteurized "fresh"
2 ounces prosciutto (1 thick slice)
5 large red bell peppers (2¼ pounds total weight)
8 spears asparagus (about ½ pound total weight)
2 medium-size carrots (about ½ pound total weight)
Small tomato (optional)
2 ounces mushrooms
Large bunch watercress
2 heads Belgian endive
Medium-size bunch parsley
Small bunch scallions
2 cloves garlic, 1 large and 1 small
8 large eggs
¼ cup milk
1 stick plus 4 tablespoons unsalted butter
1 tablespoon chicken stock, preferably homemade (see page 13), or canned
2-ounce can anchovy fillets
2-ounce jar pimientos
½ teaspoon capers
Small sour pickle
½ cup olive oil
3 tablespoons red wine vinegar
4 slices white bread
Pinch of sugar
Salt
Freshly ground pepper

UTENSILS

Food processor (optional)
Extra-large skillet
2 large skillets, one with cover
Medium-size skillet with cover
2 medium-size bowls
Small bowl
Salad spinner (optional)
Measuring cups and spoons
Chef's knife
Paring knife
Wooden fork
Wooden spoon
Metal spatula
Metal tongs
Whisk
Vegetable peeler

START-TO-FINISH STEPS

Two hours ahead: If using frozen crabmeat or shrimp for eggs recipe, set out to thaw.

1. Rinse parsley and dry with paper towels: Chop 4 table-spoons for eggs recipe and reserve 4 sprigs for garnish, if desired; mince 2 teaspoons for salad recipe. Peel garlic: Thinly slice large clove for peppers recipe; mince small clove to measure ½ teaspoon for salad recipe.
2. Follow salad recipe steps 1 and 2.
3. Follow peppers recipe step 1.
4. Follow eggs recipe steps 1 through 4.
5. While asparagus cooks, follow salad recipe step 3.
6. Follow eggs recipe steps 5 and 6.
7. While bread is sautéing, follow salad recipe step 4.
8. Follow peppers recipe steps 2 and 3.
9. While peppers are cooking, follow eggs recipe steps 7 through 11.
10. Follow salad recipe step 5, eggs recipe step 12, and serve with peppers.

RECIPES

Spanish-Style Soft-Set Eggs

2 ounces fresh crabmeat (about ⅓ cup), or 6-ounce package frozen, or 1-pound can pasteurized "fresh"
¼ pound medium-size shrimp, or 8-ounce package frozen

2 ounces mushrooms
2 ounces prosciutto (1 thick slice)
2-ounce jar pimientos
4 tablespoons chopped parsley, plus 4 sprigs for garnish (optional)
8 asparagus spears (about ½ pound total weight)
Salt
4 slices white bread
4 tablespoons plus 1 stick unsalted butter
8 large eggs
¼ cup milk
Freshly ground pepper

1. Flake crabmeat with fork. If using fresh shrimp, peel and devein. Cut shrimp in half. Wipe mushrooms with damp paper towels; trim stems, reserving for another use. Cut prosciutto into quarters.
2. If using food processor, combine mushrooms and pro-sciutto, and mince; transfer to medium-size bowl. In same manner, mince shrimp and crab, and then pimientos. Or mince all ingredients with chef's knife and place in bowl. Add chopped parsley and stir to combine.
3. Trim stems from asparagus leaving 2-inch-long spears plus tips; reserve stems for another use. Bring ½ inch water and ½ teaspoon salt to a boil over medium-high heat in medium-size skillet. Add asparagus, cover, reduce heat to medium, and simmer until just tender, 5 to 10 minutes.
4. Meanwhile, remove crusts from white bread and slice diagonally into triangles.
5. With tongs transfer asparagus to plate and cover loosely to keep warm. Dry skillet thoroughly.
6. In large skillet, heat 4 tablespoons butter over low heat. Add bread triangles and sauté, turning once, until golden and crisp on both sides, 8 to 10 minutes.
7. Transfer triangles to plate and cover with foil.
8. Break eggs into medium-size bowl and beat lightly with fork. Beat in milk and salt and pepper to taste.
9. Half fill extra-large skillet with water and bring to a boil over high heat.
10. While water is heating, melt remaining stick of butter in medium-size skillet. Add shrimp-crab mixture and sauté about 1 minute, then remove from heat.
11. Reduce boiling water to a simmer. Stir beaten eggs into shrimp-crab mixture. Gently place skillet containing egg mixture into larger skillet of simmering water to form double boiler. Stir egg mixture constantly with wooden spoon until just set but still quite soft, about 3 to 4 minutes.

12. Divide eggs among 4 plates and garnish with asparagus and parsley sprigs, if desired. Place 2 bread triangles on each side of eggs and serve.

Sauté of Red Bell Peppers

5 large red bell peppers (about 2¼ pounds total
   weight)
2 tablespoons olive oil
1 tablespoon plus 1 teaspoon thinly sliced garlic
1 tablespoon chicken stock, preferably homemade
   (see page 13), or canned
Salt
Freshly ground pepper

1. Wash peppers, dry with paper towels, core and halve, remove seeds and membranes; cut into ½-inch strips. Set aside.
2. Heat oil in large skillet. Add peppers and stir fry with wooden fork over medium-high heat 2 to 3 minutes only.
3. Reduce heat to medium, stir in garlic, chicken stock, and salt and pepper to taste. Cover, reduce heat to medium-low, and cook until peppers are crisp-tender, about 10 minutes.

Watercress, Carrot, and Endive Salad in Anchovy Vinaigrette

3 anchovy fillets
½ teaspoon capers
Small sour pickle
Small tomato (optional)
Small bunch scallions
½ teaspoon minced garlic
2 teaspoons minced parsley
¼ cup plus 2 tablespoons olive oil
3 tablespoons red wine vinegar
Pinch of sugar
Salt
Freshly ground pepper
Large bunch watercress
2 heads Belgian endive
2 medium-size carrots (about ½ pound total
   weight)

1. For vinaigrette, mince anchovy fillets. Rinse, drain, and mince capers. Mince enough pickle to measure 1 tablespoon. If using, wash tomato and dry with paper towel. Halve, core, and seed tomato; mince enough to measure 1

tablespoon. Rinse scallions, dry with paper towels, and mince enough white parts to measure 3 tablespoons plus 1 teaspoon; reserve remainder of scallions for another use.
2. In small bowl, combine anchovies, capers, pickle, tomato, scallions, garlic, parsley, olive oil, vinegar, and pinch of sugar. Whisk ingredients to blend. Add salt and pepper to taste, whisking to combine. Set aside.
3. Trim watercress of stems, wash, and dry in salad spinner or with paper towels. Wash endive, separate leaves, and dry; stack 4 endive leaves and cut into long thin strips. Repeat with remaining leaves. Peel carrots and cut diagonally into ¼-inch-thick x 2-inch-long strips. Combine carrots with endive and set aside.
4. Divide watercress among 4 salad plates, placing on one half of each plate. Place carrots and endive on other halves of plates. Cover and refrigerate until ready to serve.
5. Just before serving, whisk dressing to recombine and pour over salads.

ADDED TOUCH

If you have a chafing dish, preparing this dessert at the table would be a lovely finale to any meal. You can also serve the bananas with vanilla ice cream.

Sautéed Bananas with Pine Nuts

Small lemon
Small orange
½ cup dark brown sugar
4 tablespoons unsalted butter
4 ripe bananas
3 tablespoons Grand Marnier
2 ounces pine nuts

1. Squeeze enough lemon and orange to measure 1 teaspoon juice each. In a small bowl, mix together dark brown sugar, lemon and orange juices, and 3 tablespoons warm water.
2. Melt butter in large skillet or chafing dish over medium heat. Peel and cut bananas in half lengthwise, and then slice crosswise. Add slices to skillet and sauté 1 minute, turning once.
3. Add brown sugar mixture to skillet, reduce heat to medium-low, and cook 1 minute.
4. Stir in Grand Marnier and cook another 2 minutes, stirring occasionally.
5. Add pine nuts and stir gently to combine.
6. Divide bananas among 4 dishes and serve immediately.

Jean Anderson

MENU 1 (Right)
Eggs with Salt Cod, Onion, and Green Olives
Marinated Green Beans with Fresh Coriander
Cherry Tomatoes in Basil Butter

MENU 2
Baked Bell Peppers with Parmesan Soufflé
Shredded Zucchini and Leek Sauté
Anchovy Bread

MENU 3
Curried Eggs
Vegetable Pilaf
Stir-Fried Broccoli and Red Bell Pepper
with Fresh Ginger

World traveler, food writer, and cook Jean Anderson is a sort of culinary alchemist. Drawing upon her food-science training and her passion for exotic tastes and offbeat foods, she creates extraordinary meals from everyday ingredients. Menu 1 substantiates this: After rambling often through Portugal she discovered that the Portuguese are ingenious egg cooks with many egg recipes in their repertoire. For her entrée, she scrambles eggs with salt cod and olives—two Portuguese staples—to create a dish similar to one she ate at the Pousada do Castelo, a government inn north of Lisbon. Marinated green beans with coriander, a classic Portuguese salad, and cherry tomatoes in basil butter, an invention of her own, accompany the eggs.

Italy has inspired her Menu 2 dinner, which balances flavors, colors, shapes, and textures. Stuffed red peppers are an unexpected container for the individual main-course cheese soufflés, served with sautéed shredded vegetables, and toasted Italian bread with herbed anchovy butter.

Her Menu 3 is reminiscent of India, where she was dazzled by the array of curry spices in the markets. In this eclectic meal, she serves a curried hard-boiled egg dish based on one she sampled in the southern town of Mahabalipuram, near Madras. The addition of a vegetable pilaf and a stir-fried broccoli, red bell pepper, and fresh ginger dish (more Chinese than Indian) makes this a memorable offering.

The colors and contrasting textures in this Portuguese-inspired meal are especially vivid against simple, dark tableware. Serve each guest a wedge of eggs with salt cod along with portions of crisp marinated green beans and plump cherry tomatoes glossy with basil butter.

Eggs with Salt Cod, Onion, and Green Olives
Marinated Green Beans with Fresh Coriander
Cherry Tomatoes in Basil Butter

S alt cod is sold in large, dried slabs—with or without the skin and bones—or in small fillets, boxed or wrapped in plastic. It is available at fishmarkets or at groceries that cater to Italian, Portuguese, Greek, or Hispanic customers. Choose thick, supple pieces, preferably from the tail end of the fish. To freshen it and to remove its saltiness, salt cod must be soaked in cool water (in a nonmetallic dish) in the refrigerator the day before you plan to cook it. Change the water several times until the fish no longer tastes salty. (A cup of milk added during the final soaking helps eliminate any trace of salt.) The soaking time will vary depending on the saltiness of the cod, and pieces containing bone will require slightly more time than fillets. Remove any bones before cooking and then treat the fish as you would any fresh fish.

Fresh coriander, which is in the marinade for the green beans, is also called Chinese parsley or cilantro. A pungent, aromatic herb, it has delicate green leaves and resembles flat-leafed parsley. Select fresh-looking bunches and refrigerate coriander with its roots and stems in water. It will keep about a week.

WHAT TO DRINK

The cook suggests a red Portuguese Vinho Verde with the main course and a good Port or Madeira after dinner.

SHOPPING LIST AND STAPLES

½ pound boneless dried salt cod
1 pound green beans
1 pint cherry tomatoes
Large Spanish onion
2 small cloves garlic
Large bunch fresh coriander, or large bunch fresh parsley and ½ teaspoon coriander seeds
Small bunch fresh basil, or 2 tablespoons dried
8 large eggs
1 pint half-and-half or ½ pint light cream
6 tablespoons unsalted butter
7-ounce jar pitted green olives, preferably pimiento-stuffed
¼ cup plus 3 tablespoons olive oil, preferably extra-virgin
3 tablespoons red wine vinegar
Salt
Freshly ground pepper

UTENSILS

Food processor (optional)
Large heavy-gauge skillet, preferably enamel-lined with flameproof handle
Medium-size skillet
Large heavy-gauge saucepan with cover
Medium-size saucepan, preferably enamel-lined
Small heavy-gauge saucepan
3 medium-size bowls, one glass or porcelain
Colander
Large sieve
Salad spinner (optional)
Measuring cups and spoons
Chef's knife
Paring knife
Wooden spoon
Metal spatula
Whisk

START-TO-FINISH STEPS

The day before: Place salt cod in medium-size glass or porcelain bowl. Add 6 cups cold water, cover, and refrigerate at least 12 hours. Change water several times.

1. Follow green beans recipe steps 1 through 5.
2. Follow cod recipe steps 1 through 3.
3. Follow tomatoes recipe steps 1 through 4.
4. Follow cod recipe steps 4 through 8.
5. Follow tomatoes recipe step 5.
6. Follow cod recipe step 9.
7. Follow green beans recipe step 6, cod recipe step 10, and serve with tomatoes.

RECIPES

Eggs with Salt Cod, Onion, and Green Olives

Large Spanish onion
Small clove garlic
3 tablespoons olive oil, preferably extra-virgin
½ pound boneless dried salt cod, soaked at least 12 hours
¾ cup pitted green olives, preferably pimiento-stuffed
8 large eggs
½ cup half-and-half or light cream
Freshly ground pepper

1. Preheat oven to 200 degrees.
2. Peel onion and garlic. Cut onion into 1½-inch chunks. Place onion and garlic in processor fitted with steel blade, and chop coarsely, pulsing 4 to 5 times. Or, coarsely chop onion and garlic with chef's knife.
3. Warm olive oil over medium-low heat in large non-cast-iron skillet. Add garlic and onion and sauté 10 to 12 minutes, stirring occasionally, until soft and golden. Remove from heat and transfer skillet to oven to keep warm.
4. Drain cod and rinse well in cold water. Check that no bones are present. Place cod in medium-size saucepan, add 4 cups water, and bring to a simmer over moderate heat. Cook, uncovered, 5 minutes, or just until fish flakes easily with tip of sharp knife. Transfer cod to sieve and drain. Flake coarsely and set aside.
5. Remove skillet from oven. Set broiler rack 4 to 5 inches from heat source and preheat broiler. Halve olives lengthwise.
6. In medium-size bowl, beat together eggs, half-and-half, and pepper to taste.
7. Return skillet to medium-low heat; spread onion-garlic mixture evenly across the bottom. Pour eggs into skillet and cook, without stirring, until edges begin to set, 2 to 3 minutes.
8. Sprinkle half of cod and of olives over eggs, then stir up eggs gently from bottom to blend. Top with remaining cod and olives.
9. Place skillet in broiler and cook just until eggs are lightly set and surface is touched with brown, about 2 minutes.
10. Cut egg dish into wedges and transfer to dinner plates.

Marinated Green Beans with Fresh Coriander

Salt
1 pound green beans
Large bunch coriander, or large bunch parsley and
    ½ teaspoon coriander seeds
Small clove garlic
¼ cup olive oil, preferably extra-virgin
Pinch of freshly ground pepper
3 tablespoons red wine vinegar

1. Bring 2 quarts water and 2 teaspoons salt to a boil in large covered saucepan.
2. Trim and wash beans in tepid water. Add beans to boiling water, cover, and simmer just until crisp-tender, 8 to 10 minutes.
3. Stem enough coriander leaves or parsley to measure 1 cup. Wash leaves and dry in salad spinner or pat dry with paper towels. Peel garlic.
4. Place coriander or parsley in processor fitted with steel blade. Add garlic and chop coarsely, pulsing 4 to 5 times. Or coarsely chop coriander and garlic with chef's knife. Transfer coriander and garlic to medium-size bowl. Add olive oil, pepper and coriander seeds, if using, and toss together.
5. Drain beans, add to coriander mixture, and toss lightly.

(Do not add vinegar.) Let stand at room temperature at least 10 minutes, or until ready to serve.
6. Drizzle vinegar over beans, add salt to taste, and toss. Divide among 4 dinner plates.

Cherry Tomatoes in Basil Butter

Small bunch fresh basil, or 2 tablespoons dried
6 tablespoons unsalted butter
1 pint cherry tomatoes

1. Rinse basil, dry with paper towels, and chop enough leaves to measure 6 tablespoons.
2. In small heavy-gauge saucepan, melt butter over medium-low heat. When butter has melted, turn heat as low as possible, add basil, and leave mixture to steep 10 minutes. (If butter begins to brown, let steep off heat.)
3. Rinse tomatoes and pat dry. Set aside.
4. Pour butter into medium-size skillet. Add tomatoes, stir gently to coat, and set aside.
5. Just before serving, set skillet over very low heat. Shaking skillet gently from time to time, warm tomatoes just until heated through, about 3 minutes.

ADDED TOUCH

The garlic flavor in this rich appetizer is subdued by baking. Purée the mixture in a blender if you do not have a food processor.

Garlic-Cheese Spread with Toast Triangles

Medium-size head garlic (about 13 cloves)
½ pound Brie, Camembert, or Fontina cheese
4 tablespoons unsalted butter, chilled and cut in pats
6 slices firm-textured white bread

1. Preheat oven to 400 degrees.
2. Wrap head of garlic in double thickness heavy-duty foil and roast in oven until soft, about 35 minutes.
3. Remove garlic from oven and let cool in foil.
4. Reduce oven temperature to 325 degrees.
5. Trim rind from cheese and discard. Cut cheese into 1-inch cubes and place in top of double boiler. Set over simmering water until cheese melts, about 5 minutes.
6. Meanwhile, separate cooled garlic head into cloves. Holding a clove by pointed tip, squeeze pulp directly into food processor fitted with steel blade. Repeat with remaining garlic.
7. Start processor, add melted cheese, and then butter. Process 60 seconds nonstop. Or, combine ingredients in blender.
8. Spoon spread into a ½-cup ramekin or small crock, cover loosely, and let stand at room temperature about 1 hour before serving.
9. Stack 3 slices bread and trim off crusts. Cut slices diagonally into triangles. Repeat with remaining bread. Spread triangles on 13 x 9-inch baking sheet.
10. Place bread in oven and toast until golden brown, 5 to 7 minutes.
11. Serve toast with garlic spread.

Baked Bell Peppers with Parmesan Soufflé
Shredded Zucchini and Leek Sauté
Anchovy Bread

Fresh dill, one of the soufflé seasonings, is a feathery green herb available year-round in well-stocked supermarkets and greengrocers. Its flavor fades quickly, so it should be rinsed, then wrapped in a moist paper towel, put inside a plastic bag and refrigerated until ready to use.

WHAT TO DRINK

The best beverages with this spicy and fragrant dinner would be tea—either hot or iced—or ale.

Pale pottery with a primitive motif sets off the red peppers filled with Parmesan-cheese soufflé and the sauté of zucchini and leeks. Keep the slices of herbed anchovy bread warm in a napkin-lined bowl.

SHOPPING LIST AND STAPLES

4 large red bell peppers (each about ½ pound)
4 small zucchini (about 1 pound total weight)
4 small leeks (about 1 pound total weight)
Small yellow onion
2 medium-size cloves garlic
Small bunch fresh dill
4 large eggs
½ pint heavy cream
1 stick plus 4 tablespoons unsalted butter, approximately
½ pound Parmesan cheese
2-ounce can flat anchovy fillets packed in oil
¼ cup olive oil, preferably extra-virgin
½ teaspoon hot red pepper sauce

Long loaf Italian bread
5 slices firm-textured white bread
1 teaspoon dried oregano
1 teaspoon dried rosemary
Pinch of nutmeg, preferably freshly grated
Salt and freshly ground pepper

UTENSILS

Food processor or blender
2 large skillets
9 x 9-inch baking dish
2 small platters
2 medium-size bowls
Small bowl

Measuring cups and spoons
Chef's knife
Paring knife
Wooden spoon
Rubber spatula
Grater (if not using food processor)
Electric mixer or whisk

START-TO-FINISH STEPS

1. Follow baked peppers recipe steps 1 through 10.
2. Follow anchovy bread recipe steps 1 through 4.
3. Follow zucchini recipe steps 1 through 4.
4. Follow zucchini recipe step 5, baked peppers recipe step 11, anchovy bread recipe step 5, and serve.

RECIPES

Baked Bell Peppers with Parmesan Soufflé

½ pound Parmesan cheese
5 slices firm-textured white bread
4 large red bell peppers (each about ½ pound)
Small yellow onion
Pinch of nutmeg, preferably freshly grated
4 tablespoons unsalted butter, approximately
Small bunch fresh dill
½ teaspoon hot red pepper sauce
¾ cup heavy cream
Salt
4 large eggs

1. Preheat oven to 400 degrees.
2. If using food processor, cut Parmesan into 1½-inch cubes and process with steel blade 15 to 20 seconds to grate finely. Or, use grater to grate cheese finely. Measure 1¾ cups cheese and reserve remainder for another use.
3. Tear bread into chunks, place in processor fitted with slicing blade or in blender, and process until fine, 10 to 15 seconds. Measure 1¼ cups crumbs and reserve remainder for another use.
4. Wash peppers and pat dry with paper towels. Slice off tops; core, seed, and remove membranes. Stand peppers upright in lightly buttered baking dish. (If necessary, even bottoms by cutting off a small slice.)
5. Peel onion and mince finely. Grate nutmeg, if using fresh. Melt butter in large skillet over low heat. Add onion and nutmeg and cook, stirring occasionally, until onion is soft, about 5 minutes.
6. While onion is cooking, wash dill, dry, and chop enough to measure 2 tablespoons.
7. Remove onions from heat and add bread crumbs, cheese, red pepper sauce, cream, dill, and salt to taste, stirring to combine.
8. Separate eggs, dropping whites into medium-size bowl and blending yolks, one by one, into onion mixture.
9. Add pinch of salt to whites and, with electric mixer or whisk, beat until stiff but not dry. Fold half of whites into onion mixture, then gently but thoroughly fold in remainder. Carefully spoon about 1 cup soufflé mixture into each pepper, mounding top.
10. Bake peppers, uncovered, until soufflés are puffed and lightly browned, 20 to 25 minutes.
11. Carefully transfer peppers to platter.

Shredded Zucchini and Leek Sauté

4 small zucchini (about 1 pound total weight)
4 small leeks (about 1 pound total weight)
2 medium-size cloves garlic
¼ cup olive oil, preferably extra-virgin
Salt and freshly ground pepper

1. Wash zucchini and trim ends. Cut into 1½-inch chunks and shred, if using food processor, with medium-size shredding disk. Or, shred zucchini with grater. Turn zucchini into medium-size bowl and reserve.
2. Trim off roots and all but 1 inch of greens from leeks. Halve leeks lengthwise and wash thoroughly under cold running water. Dry with paper towels and slice crosswise. Peel garlic and mince finely.
3. Heat oil in large skillet over medium heat. Add leeks and sauté, stirring occasionally, until white part is translucent, about 3 minutes. Add zucchini and cook, stirring occasionally, just until crisp-tender, about 3 minutes.
4. Add garlic and salt and pepper to taste; toss to combine. Turn heat to very low and keep vegetables warm, uncovered, until ready to serve.
5. Transfer zucchini and leeks to platter.

Anchovy Bread

1 teaspoon dried oregano
1 teaspoon dried rosemary
2-ounce can flat anchovy fillets, undrained
1 stick unsalted butter, at room temperature
Long loaf Italian bread

1. Place oregano, rosemary, and anchovies with their oil in food processor fitted with steel blade; process 10 seconds. Scrape down sides of bowl, add butter, and process just until smooth, about 10 seconds. Or, place oregano and rosemary in a mortar and grind finely with pestle. Add anchovies and oil and mash to a paste. Transfer mixture to a small bowl, add butter, and blend with fork.
2. Using serrated knife, cut bread into 1-inch-thick slices, cutting down to—but not through—bottom crust.
3. Carefully spread slices with anchovy butter, coating both sides of each slice. Wrap loaf in aluminum foil.
4. To avoid disturbing soufflés, open oven slowly and carefully. Quickly place loaf in 400-degree oven, and then gently and slowly close door. Bake loaf 15 minutes.
5. Unwrap bread, break into clumps of several slices, and place in napkin-lined bowl.

Curried Eggs
Vegetable Pilaf
Stir-Fried Broccoli and Red Bell Pepper with Fresh Ginger

*Fragrant with exotic Indian spices, the curried eggs comple-
ment the flavors of the vegetable pilaf, garnished with fresh
coriander leaves and apple slices. Ginger-spiced broccoli and
red pepper are a bright addition.*

Curry powder is a blend of many different spices.
Indian cooks grind their own spices daily in various
combinations to suit the food being prepared. Here the
cook uses cardamom, fennel seeds, and turmeric to season
the eggs. Aromatic cardamom (with a faint lemon-eu-
calyptus flavor) is sold either as whole pods, which contain
the flavorful seeds, or as ground seeds. The pods have a
longer shelf life; remove the dark seeds and discard the
pods before using. Ground cardamom is handy but loses
both its flavor and aroma quickly. Fennel seeds have a mild
licorice flavor. Bright orange-yellow turmeric has a
slightly musky flavor, and must be used sparingly or it
imparts a bitter taste. Ground cardamom, fennel, and
turmeric are available in most supermarkets.

Fresh ginger, which is used to flavor the stir-fried broccoli and pepper, is a pale-brown gnarled root with a sharp,
sweet taste and crunchy texture. Fresh ginger should be
firm, taut-skinned, and even-colored, with no sign of
shriveling; wrinkled ginger has dried out and lacks flavor.
Powdered ginger is not a substitute.

Fresh ginger

WHAT TO DRINK

Dry white wine goes well with this Italian menu. The cook
prefers Orvieto, Soave, or Pinot Grigio, served chilled.

SHOPPING LIST AND STAPLES

Large head broccoli
Large red bell pepper, or 2 medium-size pimientos
Small carrot
Small sweet potato
Small zucchini
Large yellow onion
3 small cloves garlic
3-inch piece ginger
Small bunch fresh coriander or fresh parsley for garnish
  (optional)

Small lemon (optional)
Medium-size Granny Smith or Yellow Delicious apple,
    plus 2 for garnish (optional)
8 large eggs
1 pint half-and-half or ½ pint light cream
1 stick unsalted butter
1¾ cups chicken stock, preferably homemade
    (see page 13), or canned
¼ cup vegetable oil
2 tablespoons cider vinegar
1 cup long-grain rice
1½ teaspoons ground cardamom, preferably freshly
    ground
1 teaspoon ground cinnamon
1 teaspoon ground cloves
1 teaspoon ground coriander
1 teaspoon fennel seeds
1 teaspoon ground cumin
½ teaspoon ground turmeric
½ teaspoon Cayenne pepper
Salt
Freshly ground pepper

UTENSILS

Food processor (optional)
2 large sauté pans or heavy-gauge skillets,
    one with cover
2 medium-size heavy-gauge saucepans with covers
Medium-size bowl
Colander
Measuring cups and spoons
Chef's knife
Paring knife
Vegetable peeler
Wooden spoon
Rubber spatula
Wooden spatula
Juicer
Grater (optional)
Mortar and pestle or rolling pin
Egg slicer (optional)

START-TO-FINISH STEPS

One hour ahead: Set out 1 cup half-and-half or light cream
to bring to room temperature.

1. Follow curried eggs recipe steps 1 through 4.
2. While onions are sautéing, follow broccoli recipe steps 1
through 3.
3. Follow curried eggs recipe steps 5 and 6.
4. Follow pilaf recipe steps 1 through 3.
5. While pilaf is cooking, follow curried eggs recipe steps 7
through 10.
6. Follow broccoli recipe steps 4 and 5.
7. Follow pilaf recipe step 4, curried eggs recipe step 11,
and serve with broccoli.

Curried Eggs

8 large eggs
3 small cloves garlic
Large yellow onion
1-inch piece ginger
Medium-size Granny Smith or Yellow Delicious apple,
    plus two for garnish (optional)
4 tablespoons unsalted butter
1 teaspoon fennel seeds
1 teaspoon ground cardamom, preferably freshly
    ground
1 teaspoon ground cinnamon
1 teaspoon ground cloves
1 teaspoon ground coriander
1 teaspoon ground cumin
½ teaspoon ground turmeric
½ teaspoon Cayenne pepper
Small bunch fresh coriander or fresh parsley for garnish
    (optional)
Small lemon (optional)
1½ teaspoons salt
2 tablespoons cider vinegar
1 cup half-and-half or light cream
Vegetable Pilaf (see following recipe)

1. Place eggs in medium-size heavy-gauge saucepan, add
enough cold water to cover them by 1 inch, and bring to a
boil over high heat. Cover pan, turn off heat, and let eggs
stand 15 minutes.
2. While eggs are cooking, peel garlic, onion, and ginger.
Quarter onion. Peel, core, and quarter apple. If using food
processor, fit with steel blade and process garlic and ginger 10 seconds; scrape down work bowl sides and process
10 seconds longer. Add onion and apple and chop coarsely,
pulsing 4 to 5 times. Or, if using chef's knife, mince garlic
and ginger and coarsely chop onion and apple. Combine
ingredients in medium-size bowl.
3. Melt butter in large sauté pan over medium heat. Add
onion mixture and sauté, stirring frequently, until lightly
browned, 8 to 10 minutes.
4. Meanwhile, crush fennel seeds with mortar and pestle
or rolling pin. Grind enough cardamom seeds to measure 1
teaspoon, if using fresh.
5. Drain eggs and plunge into cold water. Immediately
crack broad end of each egg. Peel them, cover with cold
water, and set aside.
6. Reduce heat under sauté pan to low and stir in fennel
seeds, cardamom, cinnamon, cloves, coriander, cumin,
turmeric, and Cayenne pepper. Cover and cook until flavors have blended, 2 to 3 minutes. Set aside.
7. Drain eggs and pat dry. Chop eggs with chef's knife or,
using egg slicer, slice each egg lengthwise and then width-
wise. Set chopped eggs aside.
8. Prepare garnish if using: Wash coriander sprigs or
parsley and pat dry with paper towels. If using apple
slices, squeeze enough lemon juice to measure 1 table-

spoon. Wash, dry, quarter, and slice 2 apples; toss with lemon juice. Set aside coriander and apples.

9. Stir salt and vinegar into onion mixture, raise heat to medium-high, and cook, stirring constantly, until almost all liquid has evaporated, about 5 minutes.

10. Add half-and-half or cream and cook, stirring to combine, until heated through, about 2 minutes. (Mixture may look curdled but will become smooth once eggs are added). Lower heat to medium and gently stir in chopped eggs. Heat briefly, just until eggs are warm, 1 to 2 minutes. Do not let mixture boil. Cover pan and remove from heat.

11. Top each serving of pilaf with curried eggs and garnish with apple slices and coriander or parsley, if desired.

Vegetable Pilaf

Small sweet potato
Small carrot
Small zucchini
4 tablespoons unsalted butter
1 cup long-grain rice
½ teaspoon ground cardamom, preferably freshly ground
1¾ cups chicken stock
½ teaspoon salt

1. Wash vegetables and dry with paper towels. Peel sweet potato and scrape carrot. Reserve one-half sweet potato for another use. Shred sweet potato, carrot, and zucchini in food processor fitted with steel blade, or on grater.

2. Melt butter in medium-size saucepan over medium heat. Add shredded vegetables and sauté, stirring and tossing, until vegetables are coated with butter and warm. Add rice and cardamom and cook, stirring, until rice is golden, 2 to 3 minutes.

3. Add chicken stock and salt, and bring to a boil over medium-high heat. Reduce heat to a gentle simmer, cover, and cook until rice is tender and all liquid is absorbed, about 18 minutes.

4. Fluff pilaf with fork and divide among 4 dinner plates.

Stir-Fried Broccoli and Pepper with Fresh Ginger

Large head broccoli
Large red bell pepper, or 2 medium-size pimientos
2-inch piece ginger
¼ cup vegetable oil
Salt
Freshly ground pepper

1. Cut broccoli into slim florets 1½ to 2 inches long. Reserve stems for another use. You should have about 4 cups florets. Wash and shake dry.

2. Wash bell pepper and pat dry with paper towels. Halve, core, and seed pepper, and cut lengthwise into ¼-inch strips. Set aside.

3. Peel ginger and grate enough to measure 1 tablespoon; set aside.

4. In large sauté pan or heavy-gauge skillet set over high heat, heat oil until almost smoking. Add broccoli and stir fry 3 minutes. Add bell peppers and ginger and stir fry until broccoli is crisp-tender, about 2 minutes.

5. Add salt and pepper to taste and toss well.

ADDED TOUCH

Rose water, used to flavor many Indian sweets, is available at Middle Eastern stores, gourmet shops, and pharmacies.

Rose Water Pudding with Tangerine Crescents

3½ ounces marzipan
1 envelope plain gelatin
2 tablespoons superfine sugar
2 cups half-and-half or light cream
3 tablespoons rose water
1½ cups heavy cream
1½ cups fresh tangerine sections, or 11-ounce can mandarin oranges, drained
¼ cup minced blanched pistachio nuts
4 sprigs mint, washed and dried for garnish (optional)

1. Cut marzipan into small pieces. In food processor fitted with steel blade or in blender, combine marzipan, gelatin, sugar, 1 cup half-and-half or cream, and rose water. Process 20 seconds or until smooth. Add remaining half-and-half or cream and process until incorporated, 10 seconds.

2. Transfer mixture to medium-size heavy-gauge saucepan, and cook over medium-low heat, stirring often, 12 to 15 minutes, or until gelatin dissolves.

3. Chill bowl and beaters for whipping cream.

4. Fill a large bowl or saucepan with crushed ice or ice cubes and water. Set pan with marzipan mixture in ice bath for 10 to 15 minutes, being careful not to let any water spill into it. Whisk mixture frequently, until thick and syrupy.

5. With electric mixer at high speed, whip heavy cream to soft peaks, about 2 minutes, then fold into marzipan mixture. Cover pudding and chill several hours, until slightly firm, or overnight.

6. To serve, arrange tangerine sections around circumference of 4 dessert plates. Mound pudding in center of plates, scatter pistachios on top, and garnish with mint sprigs, if desired.

LEFTOVER SUGGESTION

Broccoli is a perfect partner for eggs, and you can use the leftover broccoli stems as an omelet or quiche filling. Or, create a baked egg dish by cutting up and stir frying the broccoli stems, then seasoning them with soy sauce. Layer the broccoli on the bottom of buttered individual baking dishes, add leftover rice, if you have any, and two eggs. Top with cream, butter, and salt and pepper to taste, and bake.

Arthur Schwartz

As a restaurant critic, Arthur Schwartz must dine out frequently, often at restaurants specializing in elaborate cooking. Therefore, when he cooks at home he favors casual, streamlined meals. "If I have a food philosophy," he says, "it is that the simplest meals give the most pleasure." All three of his menus are in keeping with this easy-going approach to home cooking.

In Menu 1, the Creole sauce is spooned into avocado halves to make a spicy partner for straightforward hard-boiled eggs. The cream biscuits can be made in just a few minutes and may be served with sweet butter on the side. Fresh strawberries steeped in a honey and red-wine marinade and flavored with orange rind are an aromatic and refreshing dessert. Menu 2, an Italian-style meal, features fried eggs with fresh asparagus spears and spaghetti served with an unusual garlic, olive, and cream sauce.

The egg salad with sautéed onions and mushrooms in Menu 3 is an old-fashioned Eastern European dish that was a frequent offering in the homes of Arthur Schwartz's grandmother and mother. The dried fruit compote, made with slivovitz, a plum brandy, is a suitable ethnic accompaniment. To begin the meal, the cook offers a chilled cucumber and buttermilk soup.

For a light lunch or supper serve ripe avocado halves filled with Creole sauce on beds of shredded iceberg lettuce along with hard-boiled eggs and warm biscuits. Sweet marinated strawberries are the dessert.

Avocados with Creole Sauce and Hard-Boiled Eggs
Cream Biscuits
Wine-and-Honey-Marinated Strawberries

This Louisiana-style sauce, which includes Cayenne pepper and Creole mustard, is typically served with shrimp but also complements the avocados and hard-boiled eggs. The mustard is a Louisiana specialty made from brown mustard seeds, which are given extra zip by the addition of horseradish. Creole mustard is available in specialty food shops and well-stocked supermarkets and should be refrigerated after opening.

WHAT TO DRINK

For this menu, choose a fruity red wine that you can also use in the dessert recipe. French Beaujolais, Italian Chianti, or California Zinfandel will serve equally well.

SHOPPING LIST AND STAPLES

2 medium-size avocados
Medium-size head iceberg lettuce
1 head celery
Small bunch scallions
Medium-size bunch parsley
Small orange
2 small lemons
1 quart strawberries
8 large eggs
½ pint heavy cream
4 tablespoons unsalted butter
½ cup vegetable oil
¼ cup red wine vinegar
3 tablespoons Creole mustard, or 2 tablespoons whole-grain mustard plus 2 teaspoons Dijon
4 tablespoons honey
1½ cups all-purpose flour
1 tablespoon baking powder
2 teaspoons sugar
2 tablespoons paprika
½ teaspoon Cayenne pepper, approximately
Salt
2 cups red wine, preferably Beaujolais or Zinfandel

UTENSILS

Medium-size saucepan with cover
17 x 11-inch baking sheet
3 medium-size bowls
Salad spinner (optional)

Measuring cups and spoons
Chef's knife
Paring knife
Slotted spoon
Wooden spoon
Fork
Flour sifter
Whisk

START-TO-FINISH STEPS

1. Follow strawberries recipe steps 1 through 3.
2. Follow biscuits recipe steps 1 and 2.
3. Follow eggs recipe steps 1 through 4.
4. Follow biscuits recipe step 3.
5. Follow eggs recipe steps 5 through 7, and serve with biscuits.
6. Follow strawberries recipe step 4 and serve for dessert.

RECIPES

Avocados with Creole Sauce and Hard-Boiled Eggs

2 to 3 stalks celery
Small bunch scallions
Medium-size bunch parsley
Medium-size head iceberg lettuce
8 large eggs
2 tablespoons paprika
½ teaspoon Cayenne pepper, approximately
1 teaspoon salt
3 tablespoons Creole mustard, or 2 tablespoons whole-grain mustard plus 2 tablespoons Dijon mustard
¼ cup red wine vinegar
½ cup vegetable oil
2 medium-size avocados
2 small lemons

1. Rinse celery, scallions, and parsley; dry with paper towels. Finely dice enough celery to measure 1 cup. Chop enough scallions to measure ⅓ cup. Finely chop enough parsley to measure ¾ cup.
2. Wash lettuce and dry in salad spinner or with paper towels. Cut lettuce in quarters, core, and cut into shreds. Divide lettuce among 4 dinner plates and set aside.
3. Place eggs in medium-size saucepan with enough hot

water to cover and bring to a simmer over high heat. Reduce heat and simmer eggs 8 minutes.

4. While eggs are cooking, prepare sauce: In medium-size bowl, combine paprika, Cayenne to taste, salt, mustard, vinegar, oil, scallions, celery, and parsley, and whisk until blended. Cover with plastic wrap and refrigerate.

5. When eggs are done, drain hot water from pan and add cold water to stop cooking. Peel eggs and place on paper towels to drain.

6. Halve avocados lengthwise, peel, and remove pits. Halve lemons, squeeze gently to start juices flowing, and gently rub surfaces of avocados with lemons to prevent browning. Reserve lemons for juice in strawberries recipe. Divide avocado halves among lettuce-lined plates.

7. Cut hard-boiled eggs in half and place 4 halves beside each avocado. Fill avocados with sauce.

Cream Biscuits

1½ cups all-purpose flour
1 tablespoon baking powder
2 teaspoons sugar
½ teaspoon salt
⅔ to ¾ cup heavy cream

1. Preheat oven to 425 degrees. Grease baking sheet.

2. Sift flour, baking powder, sugar, and salt together into medium-size bowl. Gradually add ⅔ cup heavy cream to flour mixture, stirring constantly with fork until dough gathers around fork. If mixture seems too dry, add a few drops of cream and stir until blended.

3. Allowing a heaping teaspoonful of dough per biscuit, use your palms to roughly form 20 to 25 flat ½-inch rounds. Place on baking sheet and bake 8 to 10 minutes, or until biscuits are puffed and lightly colored.

Wine-and-Honey-Marinated Strawberries

4 tablespoons honey
2 cups red wine, preferably Beaujolais or Zinfandel
Few drops of lemon juice (optional)
Small orange
1 quart strawberries, unhulled

1. Combine honey and ½ cup wine in medium-size bowl and stir until honey is dissolved. Add remaining wine and a few drops of lemon juice, if desired.

2. With paring knife, remove peel from orange, avoiding white pith; cut peel into 8 strips. Add 4 strips of peel to honey-wine mixture; reserve 4 for garnish.

3. Rinse unhulled berries quickly under cold running water. Shake each gently to drain and add to honey-wine mixture. Let berries stand at least 1 hour, stirring occasionally.

4. Just before serving, with slotted spoon, remove berries and orange peel from honey-wine mixture. Transfer syrup to small serving bowl. Divide berries among individual plates and garnish with orange peel.

ADDED TOUCH

This rich and satisfying stew can be prepared the night before, then covered and refrigerated. Reheat just before serving.

Oyster Stew

1 pint shucked oysters with their liquor
8-ounce bottle clam juice (optional)
2 tablespoons finely minced shallot, yellow onion, parsley, or chives, or dash of paprika or cumin (optional)
4 tablespoons unsalted butter
1 pint heavy cream
1 cup milk
Worcestershire sauce
Hot pepper sauce

1. Remove oysters from their liquor, reserving ¾ cup and adding clam juice to liquor, if necessary, to make up required measure.

2. If using minced shallot or onion for garnish, place in small bowl with cold water to cover 20 minutes before serving stew.

3. In medium-size saucepan, heat butter over medium heat just until foaming. Add oysters, stir, and reduce heat to low. When oysters begin to curl at edges, 1½ to 2 minutes, add cream, milk, ¾ cup oyster liquor, and Worcestershire and hot pepper sauces to taste. Raise heat to medium and stir mixture occasionally just until it begins to steam.

4. Remove stew from heat and let cool at room temperature, stirring occasionally. Then cover and refrigerate until needed.

5. Just before serving, remove shallot or onion garnish, if using, from water and squeeze dry with paper towels. Reheat stew just to steaming over medium heat, stirring frequently. Top stew with garnish of your choice and serve.

Fried Eggs with Asparagus
Spaghetti with Black Olive Sauce

The eggs with asparagus, topped with pan butter and freshly grated Parmesan, are accompanied by spaghetti with olive sauce.

Prepare this delightful spring brunch or light supper when asparagus is at its peak. To save preparation time, buy asparagus spears about ⅜- to ½-inch in diameter at the base, so that all the spears will cook evenly.

WHAT TO DRINK

The cook suggests a dry white Italian wine such as Pinot Grigio, Pinot Bianco, or a Tuscan white.

SHOPPING LIST AND STAPLES

24 asparagus spears (about 1½ pounds total weight)
Small clove garlic
8 large eggs
½ pint heavy cream
1 stick unsalted butter
⅓ pound Parmesan cheese, preferably imported, or other fresh grating cheese
3 ounces oil-cured black olives, or 6½-ounce jar
¾ pound spaghetti
Cayenne pepper
Salt

UTENSILS

Food processor or blender
Large stockpot or kettle with cover
Large skillet
Medium-size ovenproof bowl
Small bowl
Colander
Measuring cups and spoons
Chef's knife
Paring knife
Metal tongs
Grater (if not using processor)

START-TO-FINISH STEPS

1. Follow eggs recipe steps 1 through 4.
2. While asparagus is cooking, follow spaghetti recipe steps 1 and 2.
3. Follow eggs recipe step 5.
4. Follow spaghetti recipe steps 3 and 4.
5. Follow eggs recipe steps 6 through 9, spaghetti recipe step 5, and serve.

RECIPES

Fried Eggs with Asparagus

24 asparagus spears (about 1½ pounds total weight)
⅓ pound Parmesan cheese, preferably imported, or other fresh grating cheese
Salt
1 stick unsalted butter
8 large eggs

1. Preheat oven to 200 degrees.
2. Trim ends of asparagus and rinse under cold running water. Grate enough Parmesan to measure about 1 cup and place in small serving bowl; set aside.
3. Place asparagus in large skillet with enough cold water to barely cover; then remove asparagus while bringing water to a boil over high heat.
4. Return asparagus to skillet, add ½ teaspoon salt to water, if desired, and, as soon as water returns to a boil, reduce heat until water simmers briskly. Cook asparagus 8 minutes, or just until spears are tender but still slightly underdone. Test by cutting small slice from the base of one spear. (Spears will become more tender as they cool.)
5. With tongs, transfer asparagus to paper-towel-lined plate and drain. Transfer to heatproof platter and keep warm in oven until ready to serve.
6. Pour off water from skillet and dry. Melt 3 tablespoons butter over medium-high heat. When butter begins to foam, break in 4 eggs, spacing evenly in skillet, and fry, preferably just until whites are set and yolks are still runny. If you prefer yolks more firmly cooked, spoon a little pan butter over them. When eggs are done, divide among 2 dinner plates and place in oven.
7. Add 3 more tablespoons butter to skillet and fry remaining eggs. When done, divide eggs among 2 remaining plates and place in oven.
8. Add remaining butter to skillet, increase heat slightly, and, watching carefully to prevent butter from burning, let it foam and then brown slightly. Remove pan from heat.
9. Remove plates from oven and arrange asparagus around eggs. Spoon a little browned butter over each egg and sprinkle lightly with Parmesan. Serve with remaining grated Parmesan.

Spaghetti with Black Olive Sauce

Small clove garlic
3 ounces oil-cured black olives (about ½ cup)
½ cup heavy cream
2 tablespoons salt, approximately
Dash of Cayenne pepper
¾ pounds spaghetti

1. Peel and quarter garlic. Pit enough olives to measure about ½ cup.
2. In food processor fitted with steel blade or in blender, combine garlic, olives, and cream. Purée mixture and transfer to small bowl. Season to taste with salt and Cayenne pepper; set aside.
3. In stockpot or large kettle, bring 4 quarts water and 2 tablespoons salt to a boil, over high heat. Add spaghetti to rapidly boiling water and cook until just tender, 7 to 9 minutes. Turn into colander and drain.
4. Transfer sauce to kettle and set over medium heat. Add spaghetti and toss until evenly coated and heated through, about 2 minutes. Turn spaghetti into ovenproof bowl, cover with foil, and keep warm in oven until ready to serve.
5. Divide spaghetti among 4 side plates and serve.

Cucumber-Buttermilk Soup
Egg Salad with Sautéed Onions and Mushrooms
Dried Fruit Compote with Plum Brandy

A garnish of cucumber rounds and fresh mint leaves adds visual appeal to cool, tangy buttermilk soup. The egg salad, which contains sautéed onions and mushrooms, shares the plate with a compote of fruit macerated in plum brandy.

For the main-course egg salad, use old, dark, open-gilled mushrooms (the kind you would generally avoid buying) because they have a powerful flavor that is needed here. If you can find only young white mushrooms, intensify their flavor with a few reconstituted dried mushrooms, such as Italian porcini or French cèpes or morels. If you like, serve the egg salad with an assortment of dark breads.

WHAT TO DRINK

The flavors of this meal would be nicely matched by a simple dry white varietal wine, such as a Chardonnay or Sauvignon Blanc from Hungary or Rumania, or by a light beer or ale.

SHOPPING LIST AND STAPLES

½ pound fresh mushrooms
1 pint cherry tomatoes
Small green bell pepper
2 medium-size cucumbers (about 1 pound total weight) plus 1 for garnish (optional)
1 large onion (¾ pound total weight)
Medium-size bunch scallions
Small bunch radishes
Small bunch mint for garnish (optional)
Medium-size clove garlic
Small lemon
7¼-ounce can black olives
1 dozen large eggs
1 quart low-fat buttermilk
4 tablespoons unsalted butter, or butter and vegetable oil combined
½ ounce dried wild mushrooms, approximately (optional)
¾ pound pitted prunes (about 1½ cups), or 1-pound box
15-ounce box golden raisins
8-ounce package dried apricots (about ½ cup)
Salt and freshly ground pepper
2 tablespoons slivovitz, kirsch, or other fruit brandy

UTENSILS

Food processor or blender
Medium-size skillet
Large saucepan with cover
Medium-size saucepan with cover
Large bowl

Small bowl or cup (optional)
Measuring cups and spoons
Chef's knife
Paring knife
Wooden spoon
Slotted spoon
Vegetable peeler (optional)
Wooden bowl and chopper (optional)

START-TO-FINISH STEPS

1. Follow egg salad recipe step 1.
2. Follow soup recipe steps 1 through 3.
3. Follow compote recipe steps 1 and 2.
4. Follow egg salad recipe steps 2 through 9.
5. Follow soup recipe step 4, compote recipe step 3, and serve with egg salad.

RECIPES

Cucumber-Buttermilk Soup

2 medium-size cucumbers (about 1 pound total weight)
    plus 1 for garnish (optional)
4 mint sprigs for garnish (optional)
Medium-size clove garlic
1 quart low-fat buttermilk
Salt

1. Rinse cucumbers and pat dry with paper towels. Peel 2 cucumbers and cut in half lengthwise. Scoop out seeds with teaspoon and discard; cut into chunks. If using additional cucumber for garnish, rinse and dry with paper towels. Cut in half crosswise; reserve one half for another use. Without peeling, cut remaining half into 8 slices and set aside. If using mint for garnish, rinse 4 sprigs and dry.
2. Peel garlic and chop enough to measure 1 to 2 teaspoons.
3. Prepare soup in two batches: In food processor fitted with steel blade or in blender, combine half the cucumber chunks, half the buttermilk, ½ to 1 teaspoon garlic, salt to taste, and 2 ice cubes, and process just until ice is dissolved and mixture is frothy, about 30 seconds. Divide soup between 2 bowls. Repeat with remaining ingredients. Cover and refrigerate soup until ready to serve.
4. Just before serving, float 2 cucumber slices in each bowl and garnish with mint sprig, if desired.

Egg Salad with Sautéed Onions and Mushrooms

¼ to ½ ounce dried wild mushrooms (optional)
1 dozen large eggs
1 large onion (¾ pound total weight)
½ pound fresh mushrooms
Small green bell pepper
4 cherry tomatoes
8 scallions
4 radishes

4 tablespoons unsalted butter, or butter and vegetable oil combined
Salt
Freshly ground pepper
12 black or purple olives

1. If using dried mushrooms, place in small bowl or cup with enough hot water to cover; set aside.
2. Place eggs in large saucepan with enough hot water to cover. Cover pan and bring to a simmer, over high heat. Remove cover and cook eggs 8 minutes.
3. While eggs are cooking, peel onions and chop enough to measure 1½ cups. Wipe fresh mushrooms with damp paper towels, trim stems, and chop coarsely; set aside. To prepare garnishes: Halve pepper, reserving one half for another use; core, seed, and remove membranes from remaining half. Cut 4 thin lengthwise strips from pepper, or more if desired, reserving any remaining pepper for another use. Wash and dry cherry tomatoes. Wash, trim, and dry scallions and radishes. Slice radishes thinly.
4. When eggs are done, drain, plunge into cold water, and shell. Place on paper towels to dry.
5. Heat butter in medium-size skillet set over medium-low heat. Add onions and sauté, stirring occasionally, until soft and translucent, 7 to 10 minutes.
6. While onions are cooking, chop each egg over large bowl. Holding paring knife in one hand and egg in the other, slice egg lengthwise into eighths, then crosswise into small chunks. Or, chop coarsely in wooden bowl with chopper.
7. If using dried mushrooms, drain, reserving liquid for another use, and chop coarsely.
8. Add fresh and dried mushrooms to sautéed onions in skillet, stirring to combine. When fresh mushrooms begin exuding liquid, raise heat to medium-high and sauté, stirring, until pan juices have completely evaporated, about 3 to 4 minutes. Remove pan from heat.
9. Add chopped eggs and salt and pepper to taste to sautéed mushrooms and onions; toss to combine. Divide egg mixture among individual plates and garnish with green pepper strips, cherry tomato, scallions, radish slices, and olives.

Dried Fruit Compote with Plum Brandy

Small lemon
¾ pound pitted prunes (1½ cups), or 1-pound box
3 ounces dried apricots (about ½ cup)
⅔ cup golden raisins
2 tablespoons slivovitz, kirsch, or other fruit brandy

1. Rinse lemon and pat dry; cut two ½-inch-wide strips of peel. Reserve remainder of lemon for another use.
2. In medium-size saucepan, combine prunes, apricots, raisins, and lemon peel with just enough water to cover. Cover pan and bring to a boil over high heat. Cook fruit 1 to 2 minutes, or just until softened. Remove pan from heat and let cool, stirring fruit occasionally.
3. Just before serving, stir in slivovitz. With slotted spoon, divide fruit among plates.

Elizabeth Alston

Elizabeth Alston admires the food of many countries, as evidenced by her egg menus, which draw upon American, French, and Italian cuisines. She also specializes in simplifying complicated recipes—whatever their source. "I am always trying to cut back on the hours, the pots and pans, and the steps involved in a recipe," she says. "People want tasty food, but they don't have hours to prepare it."

Her broccoli *roulade* in Menu 2 is an example of a trimmed-down recipe. A classic egg *roulade* is a flat soufflé that normally requires about 20 minutes baking time before it is filled and rolled. Her version cooks on top of the stove in a skillet for about 2 minutes and is then filled with a creamy mixture of broccoli, Parmesan, and ricotta. In Menu 3 she prepares a *frittata* that is a variation on the traditional flat, open-faced Italian omelet. Flavored with coriander and containing chunks of avocado, this frittata does not require turning and is served directly from the pan.

In Menu 1 Elizabeth Alston adapts an American favorite—cheese bake—by using smoked Gouda to give added flavor. The smoky taste of this substantial dish is countered by a refreshing sweet-and-sour carrot salad.

For an informal brunch or light supper, serve a baked pinwheel of French bread, smoked Gouda, diced ham, and scallions accompanied by a marinated carrot salad and an assortment of toasted bagels.

85

Ham and Smoked Cheese Bake
Sweet-and-Sour Carrot Salad

The ham and smoked cheese bake is a variation of an American standby known as a strata (a layered casserole), which was probably devised to use up stale bread. This dish is ideal for busy people because it is best when assembled several hours in advance, or even the night before, then covered and refrigerated before baking. The lengthy soaking allows the ham and cheese to flavor the milk, but the dish can also be prepared without the advance soaking.

Instead of smoked Gouda, you can use smoked Cheddar or smoked mozzarella, but buy only naturally smoked cheese. Be sure to slice off any rind because it toughens during baking. Four slices of plain white bread are an alternative to the French or Italian bread.

WHAT TO DRINK

This meal can be accompanied by a dry, fruity white or red wine. If you prefer white, try an Italian Soave or Pinot Grigio; for red, choose a young French Beaujolais or California Gamay Beaujolais.

SHOPPING LIST AND STAPLES

¼ pound baked ham
1½ pounds carrots
Small head Bibb lettuce
Small bunch scallions
Small bunch parsley
2 medium-size lemons
4 large eggs
1½ cups milk
1 tablespoon unsalted butter, approximately
¼ pound smoked Gouda or other smoked cheese
8-ounce loaf long French or Italian bread, preferably, or other white bread
6 assorted bagels
5½-ounce bag hazelnuts (optional)
2 tablespoons sugar
½ teaspoon dry mustard
¼ teaspoon paprika
Salt and freshly ground black pepper

UTENSILS

1½-quart shallow baking dish, preferably round
Serving platter

2 medium-size bowls
Salad spinner (optional)
Measuring cups and spoons
Chef's knife
Paring knife
Serrated knife
Wooden spoon
Rubber spatula
Vegetable peeler
Grater
Juicer
Whisk

START-TO-FINISH STEPS

The evening before: If desired, follow ham and cheese bake recipe steps 1 through 5.

1. Follow ham and cheese bake recipe steps 1 through 6, if not already prepared, or just follow step 6.
2. Follow carrot salad recipe step 1.
3. Follow ham and cheese bake recipe step 7.
4. Follow carrot salad recipe steps 2 through 4.
5. Follow ham and cheese bake recipe steps 8 and 9, carrot salad recipe step 5, and serve.

RECIPES

Ham and Smoked Cheese Bake

1 tablespoon unsalted butter, approximately
8-ounce loaf long French or Italian bread, preferably, or other white bread
¼ pound smoked Gouda or other smoked cheese
¼ pound baked ham
Small bunch scallions
4 large eggs
1½ cups milk
½ teaspoon dry mustard
¼ teaspoon paprika
½ teaspoon freshly ground black pepper
⅛ teaspoon salt (optional)
6 assorted bagels

1. Butter 1½-quart shallow baking dish.
2. Trim loaf and discard ends. Cut loaf into 16 slices and arrange overlapping slices in baking dish (see following illustration).

Arrange overlapping slices of bread in baking dish.

Pour egg mixture over bread, cheese, ham, and scallions.

3. Trim rind from cheese. Grate enough cheese to measure about 1 cup. Chop ham finely. Trim scallions, rinse, and pat dry. Chop enough scallions to measure ⅓ cup, using some of green.

4. Sprinkle cheese over bread and top with ham and scallions.

5. Combine eggs, milk, mustard, paprika, pepper, and salt, if using, in medium-size bowl. Beat mixture until blended and then pour over bread. Press bread down into egg to submerge it and let sit 5 minutes, or cover and refrigerate overnight.

6. Preheat oven to 350 degrees.

7. Place baking dish on rack in middle of oven and bake until lightly browned and set, 35 to 45 minutes.

8. Remove ham and cheese bake from oven and let stand 5 minutes before serving.

9. Cut bagels in half and toast lightly.

Sweet-and-Sour Carrot Salad

1½ pounds carrots
2 medium-size lemons
¼ teaspoon freshly ground black pepper

2 tablespoons sugar
Small head Bibb lettuce
Small bunch parsley
1 tablespoon shelled hazelnuts for garnish (optional)

1. Trim and scrape carrots; coarsely grate enough to measure about 6 cups. Squeeze enough lemon juice to measure about ½ cup.

2. Mix pepper, sugar, and lemon juice to taste in a medium-size bowl, stirring until sugar is dissolved. Add carrots and toss to coat well. Cover and refrigerate until ready to serve, tossing once or twice.

3. Wash lettuce and parsley and dry in salad spinner or pat dry with paper towels. Line serving platter with lettuce leaves, cover with plastic wrap, and refrigerate. Chop enough parsley to measure 1 tablespoon.

4. If using hazelnuts, chop enough to measure 1 tablespoon and set aside.

5. Toss carrots and mound on top of lettuce. Sprinkle with parsley and hazelnuts, if using.

___

ADDED TOUCH

A brief cooking in sugar syrup, rather than water, helps to preserve the texture of the apricots. Save any leftover syrup and use it for poaching other fruit, such as apples or bananas.

Poached Apricots with Almonds

½ cup sugar
1 cup dried apricot halves
3 tablespoons apricot or orange liqueur
¼ cup toasted sliced almonds
½ to ¾ cup heavy cream, or crème fraîche (optional)

1. Bring sugar and 2 cups water to a boil in large stainless steel skillet, stirring once or twice to dissolve sugar. Reduce heat and simmer 1 minute.

2. Add apricots to sugar syrup, stir, and return syrup to a simmer. Cover skillet and cook apricots 5 to 8 minutes. Apricots should be plump but still chewy.

3. Remove skillet from heat and stir in liqueur. Cover and let stand at room temperature approximately 1 hour.

4. Transfer apricots and syrup to serving bowl. Cover and chill at least 2 hours.

5. Divide apricots among 4 bowls and sprinkle with toasted almonds. If desired, serve with heavy cream or crème fraîche.

Broccoli Roulade with Tomato Sauce
Sesame Pita Rounds

Select a skillet that measures 9 to 10 inches across the bottom and has sloping sides, so you can remove the eggs easily. They cook quickly but require your undivided attention. Read the recipe a few times to become thoroughly familiar with the method, and be sure to have your utensils—including the oven mitts and the plate or baking sheet—handy. When you turn the eggs out after finishing cooking, you may find that the edges of the pancake are a bit crusty. If so, trim the crust so that it does not crack when you roll it.

Thyme-flavored, freshly made tomato sauce forms a base for slices of roulade, *here a rolled egg "pancake soufflé" with a broccoli and cheese filling. The sesame pita breads are buttered, then baked until golden.*

WHAT TO DRINK

Choose a red or white wine that is crisp and acidic: a French Muscadet for white or Italian Barbera for red.

SHOPPING LIST AND STAPLES

Small head broccoli
Small onion
Small clove garlic
28-ounce can peeled plum tomatoes in tomato purée
5 large eggs
4½ tablespoons unsalted butter, approximately
8-ounce container whole-milk ricotta cheese

¼ pound Parmesan cheese
1 tablespoon plus 1 teaspoon olive oil
2 teaspoons flour
4 pita breads with sesame seeds, each about 6 inches in
 diameter
½ teaspoon dried thyme
¼ teaspoon nutmeg
Salt
Freshly ground pepper

UTENSILS

Food processor (optional)
12-inch nonstick skillet
Large heavy-gauge skillet with cover

Small skillet
Medium-size heavy-gauge stainless steel saucepan with
 cover
Large round plate or baking sheet, at least 12 inches wide
17 x 11-inch baking sheet
2 medium-size bowls, preferably one metal
Small bowl
Colander
Sieve
Measuring cups and spoons
Chef's knife
Paring knife
Wooden spoon
Metal spatula
2 rubber spatulas

Grater
Large balloon whisk, rotary beater, or electric mixer
Pastry brush
Oven mitts or potholders

START-TO-FINISH STEPS

1. Follow tomato sauce recipe steps 1 through 5.
2. While tomato sauce is simmering, follow roulade recipe steps 1 through 6.
3. Follow pita recipe steps 1 through 3.
4. Cover sauce, remove pan from heat, and follow roulade recipe steps 7 through 14.
5. Follow pita recipe step 4 and serve with roulade.

RECIPES

Broccoli Roulade with Tomato Sauce

2 to 3 stalks broccoli
2½ ounces Parmesan cheese
1½ tablespoons unsalted butter, approximately
5 large eggs
2 teaspoons flour
¾ teaspoon salt
¼ teaspoon freshly ground black pepper
¼ teaspoon nutmeg
1 cup whole-milk ricotta cheese
Tomato Sauce (see following recipe)

1. Wash broccoli and shake dry. Remove florets and set aside. Trim stems, peel, and cut into 1-inch chunks. Add enough stem pieces to florets to measure about 4 cups.
2. In food processor fitted with steel blade, or with chef's knife, finely chop broccoli.
3. Bring ½ cup water to a simmer in large heavy-gauge skillet. Add broccoli, stir, cover pan, and cook until tender but still crisp, 3 to 4 minutes.
4. Drain broccoli in colander and gently pat dry; set aside.
5. Grate enough Parmesan cheese to measure about ½ cup.
6. Butter 12-inch-wide round plate or baking sheet.
7. Separate eggs, placing whites in medium-size metal bowl and yolks in small bowl. Stir flour, ¼ teaspoon salt, and ⅛ teaspoon each of pepper and nutmeg into egg whites. Whip whites until just stiff enough to leave a trail when beater is raised. Scrape down sides of bowl. Add yolks and whisk just until evenly pale yellow.
8. Combine ricotta, Parmesan cheese, ½ teaspoon salt, and remaining pepper and nutmeg in skillet used for broccoli. Set skillet over lowest possible heat and warm mixture, stirring occasionally. Do not permit filling to become very hot or it will turn watery.
9. Warm 12-inch nonstick skillet over very low heat; add 1½ tablespoons butter.
10. Meanwhile, add broccoli to ricotta mixture and continue to warm over very low heat, stirring occasionally.
11. Increase heat to medium-low under nonstick skillet and carefully add egg mixture, using rubber spatula to spread mixture evenly out to sides of pan. Cook until mixture starts to bubble and heave slightly and eggs have begun to set, 1 to 2 minutes. Remove pan from heat.
12. Using metal spatula, ease eggs out onto buttered plate. Turn empty skillet over eggs. Wearing oven mitts or using potholders to protect your hands, hold skillet and plate firmly together and invert so eggs fall back into pan, uncooked side down. Return skillet to heat for about 30 seconds. Again cover pan with plate and invert so eggs fall onto plate.
13. Scoop warmed cheese and broccoli filling onto egg pancake, distributing evenly, and leaving a 1-inch margin so the filling does not ooze out when rolled. Fold pancake over filling and then fold again, jelly-roll style.
14. Place about ½ cup tomato sauce on each of 4 plates. Cut roulade into 8 slices and place 2 slices on top of sauce on each plate.

Tomato Sauce

Small onion
Small clove garlic
1 tablespoon plus 1 teaspoon olive oil
28-ounce can peeled plum tomatoes in tomato purée
½ teaspoon dried thyme
Salt and freshly ground black pepper

1. Peel onion and chop enough to measure about ¼ cup. Peel and mince garlic.
2. Place olive oil in medium-size heavy-gauge stainless steel saucepan set over medium-low heat. Add onion and garlic, and cook, stirring occasionally, until tender, about 5 minutes.
3. While onion is cooking, drain tomatoes in sieve set over medium-size bowl and let sit 4 to 5 minutes.
4. Add thyme and drained tomatoes to saucepan, crushing tomatoes with back of wooden spoon. Using rubber spatula, scrape tomato purée off sieve and add to pan. Reserve tomato juices for another use.
5. Set sauce over medium-high heat and bring to a simmer, stirring frequently. Reduce heat to medium and cook, stirring occasionally, using spoon to crush tomatoes into smaller pieces. When sauce has thickened and flavors are well blended, 10 to 15 minutes, remove from heat and add salt and pepper to taste.

Sesame Pita Rounds

3 tablespoons unsalted butter
4 pita breads with sesame seeds, each about 6 inches in diameter

1. Preheat oven to 350 degrees.
2. Melt butter in small skillet over low heat.
3. Split pita breads horizontally so each becomes 2 rounds. Using about half of butter, brush outside of each pita and arrange breads on 17 x 11-inch baking sheet in single layer. Bake until crisp and lightly browned, 8 to 10 minutes.
4. Brush insides of pita breads with remaining butter.

Chili Peanuts
Avocado and Fresh Coriander Frittata / Crunchy Tortilla Triangles
Snow Pea, Endive, and Lettuce Salad

Chili peanuts will whet appetites for the avocado frittata, *which is served with a tossed salad and warm tortilla triangles.*

The delicate main-course *frittata* cooks only on one side because direct high heat would ruin the texture and flavor of the avocado filling. The top will set after you remove the eggs from the heat because they continue to cook for a few moments.

WHAT TO DRINK

You could serve iced margaritas before this spicy meal. A dark beer or a soft, fruity white California Chenin Blanc could also precede and accompany the *frittata*.

SHOPPING LIST AND STAPLES

¼ pound snow peas
Medium-size firm avocado
Small head leaf lettuce, or small bunch watercress
2 medium-size Belgian endives
Small bunch coriander
8 large eggs
6-ounce container plain yogurt
4 tablespoons unsalted butter
3 tablespoons olive or vegetable oil
1 tablespoon red wine vinegar or rice vinegar

¼ teaspoon soy sauce
¼ teaspoon Dijon mustard
16-ounce jar roasted, salted peanuts
6 to 8 fresh corn tortillas, preferably, or
    1 package frozen
3 teaspoons ground cumin, approximately
2 tablespoons chili powder, approximately
Salt
Freshly ground black pepper

UTENSILS

Large skillet, preferably nonstick or well-seasoned,
    with cover
Small skillet
Medium-size saucepan
17 x 11-inch baking sheet
9 x 7-inch baking sheet
Large bowl
Medium-size bowl
Colander
Cup
Salad spinner (optional)
Measuring cups and spoons
Chef's knife
Paring knife
Metal spatula or pie server
Pastry brush

START-TO-FINISH STEPS

One hour ahead: If using frozen tortillas for triangles, set
out to thaw.

1. Follow peanuts recipe step 1.
2. Follow salad recipe steps 1 through 3.
3. Follow peanuts recipe step 2.
4. While peanuts are heating, follow salad recipe steps 4
through 6.
5. Follow peanuts recipe step 3 and serve as appetizer.
6. Follow frittata recipe steps 1 and 2.
7. Follow tortilla triangles recipe steps 1 through 5.
8. While triangles are baking, follow frittata recipe steps 3
through 5.
9. While frittata is setting, follow tortilla triangles recipe
step 6.
10. Follow frittata recipe step 6.

11. Follow salad recipe step 7 and serve with frittata and
tortilla triangles.

RECIPES

Chili Peanuts

2 cups roasted, salted peanuts
1 to 2 teaspoons chili powder

1. Preheat oven to 250 degrees.
2. Place peanuts on 9 x 7-inch baking sheet and bake 5 to 7
minutes or until heated through.
3. Transfer peanuts to serving dish, sprinkle with chili
powder to taste, and toss to coat evenly.

Avocado and Fresh Coriander Frittata

Small bunch coriander, or 1 tablespoon chili powder
8 large eggs
½ cup plain yogurt
½ teaspoon salt
¼ teaspoon freshly ground black pepper
½ to 1 teaspoon ground cumin
2 tablespoons unsalted butter
Medium-size firm avocado

1. Wash coriander, pat dry with paper towels, and chop
enough to measure 2 tablespoons.
2. Break eggs into medium-size bowl and beat just until
blended. Add yogurt, salt, pepper, and cumin to taste, and
beat thoroughly with whisk. Stir in coriander.
3. Set large well-seasoned or nonstick skillet over medium
heat. Add butter and, when frothy, pour in egg mixture.
Cover pan, raise heat to medium-high, and cook eggs,
without stirring, until almost set but still very creamy on
top, about 5 minutes.
4. While eggs are cooking, peel and pit avocado, and cut
into ½-inch chunks. You should have about 1¼ cups.
5. Sprinkle avocado over frittata, cover, and cook 3 to 5
minutes.
6. Remove from heat, still covered, and let stand until top
is set but not dry, 2 to 3 minutes. Cut into wedges.

Crunchy Tortilla Triangles

2 tablespoons unsalted butter
6 to 8 fresh corn tortillas, preferably, or 6 to 8 frozen
    tortillas, thawed

1 to 2 teaspoons ground cumin or chili powder,
   approximately
Salt

1. Preheat oven to 350 degrees.
2. Melt butter in small skillet over low heat.
3. Brush tortillas lightly with melted butter. Sprinkle one side of each tortilla lightly with either cumin or chili powder and salt to taste.
4. Stack tortillas and cut into 4 wedges. Spread tortilla triangles in single layer on ungreased 17 x 11-inch baking sheet.
5. Bake triangles, turning once or twice, until crisp and lightly browned, about 10 minutes. Watch carefully to make sure they do not burn.
6. Remove triangles from oven and transfer to napkin-lined basket.

Snow Pea, Endive, and Lettuce Salad

½ cup snow peas
Small head leaf lettuce, or small bunch watercress
2 medium-size Belgian endive
3 tablespoons olive or vegetable oil
1 tablespoon red wine vinegar or rice vinegar
¼ teaspoon salt
¼ teaspoon soy sauce
Freshly ground black pepper
¼ teaspoon Dijon mustard

1. Bring 1 quart water to a boil in medium-size saucepan over high heat.
2. Trim ends of snow peas. Rinse and drain pods.
3. Add snow peas to boiling water and cook over high heat exactly 30 seconds. Transfer to colander and immediately refresh under cold running water. Drain snow peas and pat dry with paper towels.
4. Trim lettuce or watercress of yellowed leaves. Wash and dry greens and tear into bite-size pieces.
5. Rinse endive, remove any bruised portions, and pat dry with paper towels. Cutting on the diagonal, slice endive into 1-inch pieces. Separate sections.
6. Combine snow peas, salad greens, and endive in large bowl, cover, and refrigerate.
7. Pour oil over salad and toss until evenly coated. Combine remaining ingredients in cup and beat with fork until blended. Add to salad and toss again until well-mixed. Transfer salad to large platter.

The prune purée gives body to this light mousse, so that it does not require whipped cream. Beat the egg whites just until they form soft peaks; do not overbeat, or the mousse may become grainy.

Armagnac Prune Mousse with Crème de la Crème

8-ounce box pitted prunes
1 tea bag
2 teaspoons unflavored gelatin
3 to 4 tablespoons Armagnac or Cognac
1 tablespoon vanilla extract
2 large eggs
8-ounce container sour cream
8-ounce container plain yogurt

1. Place 1¼ cups prunes in small heavy-gauge saucepan, add 1 cup water, and bring to a boil over medium-high heat.
2. Remove pan from heat, add tea bag to prunes and water, and let steep 2 minutes.
3. Remove tea bag and bring mixture to a boil. Reduce to a simmer, cover, and cook prunes until quite soft, 15 minutes.
4. Sprinkle gelatin over ¼ cup cold water and let stand about 3 minutes.
5. Stir gelatin into hot prunes until dissolved. Transfer prunes and liquid to bowl of food processor and purée until very smooth. Or, push prunes through fine disk of food mill.
6. Transfer purée to large bowl, add Armagnac or Cognac and vanilla, and stir until blended. With rubber spatula, spread purée up sides of bowl to hasten cooling and leave 15 to 20 minutes.
7. Separate eggs, placing whites in small, deep bowl and reserving yolks for another use. Beat whites with electric mixer at high speed just until soft peaks form, 1 to 2 minutes.
8. Stir about half of whites into prune mixture. Scrape down sides of bowl and, still using rubber spatula, fold in remaining whites.
9. Transfer mixture into serving bowl or divide among 4 individual dishes. Cover and refrigerate at least 2 hours before serving.
10. To make Crème de la Crème, combine sour cream and yogurt and stir until blended.
11. Serve mousse accompanied by Crème de la Crème.

Rowena Hubbard

Rowena Hubbard avows that cooking is a joy for her. "It has been part of my personal and professional life for as long as I can remember," she says. Over the years, she has learned to avoid highly seasoned or elaborate recipes and to focus on meals that are light and easy to prepare. She prefers to key her menus to seasonal produce, using whatever looks best in the market. Her Menu 1 is a cold-weather meal featuring a hot first-course consommé and a main course of *gougère* (a *pâte à chou*, or cream-puff pastry incorporating cheese), filled with a mixture of spinach and clams.

In San Francisco, where Rowena Hubbard lives, crab boats unloading their catch on the wharves are the first sign that winter is over. She celebrates spring in Menu 2 with crabmeat custards, supplementing them with brown rice and a cauliflower salad flavored with sesame oil. In Menu 3, she simmers fresh tomatoes and basil with sherry and saffron for a height-of-summer soup. Her garden harvest *frittata* is baked rather than cooked on top of the stove and contains a variety of fresh vegetables in season, including zucchini, fresh peas, and red and green bell peppers.

Sherry-spiked consommé garnished with orange slices and chopped chives sets the stage for a platter of gougère *filled with a clam and spinach cream. Tomatoes and coriander dressed with mellow balsamic vinegar accompany the main course.*

Sherried Consommé with Oranges
Parmesan Gougère with Spinach-Clam Cream Sauce
Tomato and Fresh Coriander Salad

To make the *gougère* foolproof: Add the flour to the boiling water-butter mixture all at once and stir vigorously just until the paste forms a smooth ball and no longer clings to the spoon. Then remove the pan from the heat immediately. Incorporate the room-temperature eggs one by one. The dough is the right consistency if it holds its shape when lifted with a spoon.

WHAT TO DRINK

The best accompaniment for a *gougère* is a dry white wine; try a California Sauvignon Blanc or a Pouilly-Fumé.

SHOPPING LIST AND STAPLES

2 bunches spinach (about ½ pound total weight)
2 medium-size tomatoes (about 1 pound total weight)
Large bunch fresh coriander
Small onion
Small bunch chives
Large orange
4 large eggs
½ pound Parmesan cheese
1 to 1½ cups milk
1 pint half-and-half
1 stick unsalted butter
Two 10½-ounce cans consommé
Two 6½-ounce cans chopped clams
¼ cup olive oil
¼ cup balsamic vinegar
1½ cups flour
¼ teaspoon plus pinch of nutmeg
Salt and freshly ground pepper
¼ cup medium-dry sherry

UTENSILS

Large saucepan with cover
Medium-size saucepan
Small saucepan
13 x 9-inch baking sheet
Colander
Salad spinner (optional)
Measuring cups and spoons
Chef's knife
Paring knife
Wooden spoon
Ladle

Teaspoon
Rubber spatula
Metal spatula
Grater
Scissors

START-TO-FINISH STEPS

1. Follow salad recipe steps 1 through 4.
2. Follow cream sauce recipe steps 1 through 7.
3. Follow gougère recipe steps 1 through 8.
4. While gougère is baking, follow consommé recipe steps 1 through 5 and serve.
5. Follow cream sauce recipe step 8, gougère recipe steps 9 and 10, salad recipe step 5, and serve.

RECIPES

Sherried Consommé with Oranges

Two 10½-ounce cans consommé
Large orange
¼ cup medium-dry sherry
Small bunch chives

1. Bring consommé and 1 cup water to a boil in small saucepan.
2. Cut orange crosswise into four ½-inch-thick center slices. Remove pits. Cut slices in half and place 2 halves in each of 4 small soup bowls.
3. Spoon about 1 tablespoon sherry over each serving.
4. Wash chives and dry with paper towels. Snip to measure 2 teaspoons.
5. Ladle hot consommé into bowls. Garnish each with ½ teaspoon chopped chives.

Parmesan Gougère with Spinach-Clam Cream Sauce

½ pound Parmesan cheese
6 tablespoons unsalted butter
1 cup flour
Pinch of salt and freshly ground pepper
Pinch of nutmeg
4 large eggs
Spinach-Clam Cream Sauce (see following recipe)

1. Preheat oven to 400 degrees.
2. Grate Parmesan cheese to measure about 1½ cups.

3. Combine butter and 1 cup water in medium-size saucepan. Bring to a boil over high heat.

4. Add flour, salt, pepper, and nutmeg all at once, stirring until mixture forms a smooth compact mass. Remove from heat.

5. Add eggs one at a time, beating vigorously after each addition to blend thoroughly.

6. Beat in grated cheese until completely incorporated.

7. Drop dough by heaping tablespoons onto a well-greased baking sheet, so that spoonfuls just touch each other and form a ring (you should have about 10 mounds). Round mounds with back of spoon if necessary.

8. Bake gougère 35 to 40 minutes, or until puffed and browned.

9. Cool gougère 5 minutes, then cut off tops of puffs and reserve. Using a teaspoon, fill each puff with Spinach-Clam Cream Sauce and arrange in circle on serving platter. Replace tops.

10. Spoon remaining cream sauce into center of circle and serve immediately.

Spinach-Clam Cream Sauce

2 bunches spinach (about ½ pound total weight)
Small onion
Two 6½-ounce cans chopped clams
1 to 1½ cups milk
2 tablespoons unsalted butter
½ cup flour
½ cup half-and-half
¼ teaspoon nutmeg
Salt and freshly ground pepper

1. Stem spinach and wash leaves thoroughly. Drain but do not dry.

2. Transfer spinach to large saucepan, cover, and steam over medium-high heat about 2 minutes, or just until wilted. Drain thoroughly, chop coarsely, and set aside to cool briefly.

3. Peel onion and chop enough to measure ½ cup.

4. Drain clams, reserving liquid in measuring cup; add milk to liquid to measure total of 2 cups.

5. Melt butter over medium-high heat in saucepan in which spinach cooked. Sauté onion until translucent, 4 to 5 minutes.

6. Stir flour into onion. Add milk-clam juice mixture, half-and-half, nutmeg, and salt and pepper to taste. Cook 3 to 4 minutes, stirring constantly, until thickened.

7. Remove sauce from heat and stir in clams and spinach. Cover and set aside.

8. Before serving, set over medium heat 2 or 3 minutes, just until heated through.

Tomato and Fresh Coriander Salad

1 large bunch fresh coriander
2 medium-size tomatoes (about 1 pound total weight)
¼ cup olive oil
¼ cup balsamic vinegar
¼ teaspoon salt
Freshly ground black pepper

1. Wash and trim coriander; dry in salad spinner or with paper towels. Arrange on platter.

2. Wash and dry tomatoes; cut crosswise into ¼-inch-thick slices. Arrange over coriander.

3. Beat olive oil with vinegar and salt. Spoon dressing over tomatoes.

4. Cover salad with plastic wrap and chill until just before serving.

5. Sprinkle with pepper to taste and serve with main course.

ADDED TOUCH

Crème de cassis, a sweet black-currant liqueur, turns the whipped cream a rosy color. Instead of oranges, you can use hulled and halved strawberries or bananas cut into bite-size pieces.

Fresh Oranges with Cassis Cream

2 large navel oranges
¼ cup sugar
1 cup heavy cream
½ teaspoon grated orange peel
2 tablespoons crème de cassis

1. Chill bowl and beaters for whipping cream.

2. Peel oranges, removing all white pith. Separate into segments, then cut into bite-size pieces.

3. Gradually adding sugar, whip cream at medium-high speed 2 to 3 minutes, or until soft peaks form.

4. Sprinkle in grated orange peel and crème de cassis; whip cream until stiff peaks form, about 1 minute. Fold in orange segments.

5. Dessert may be served at once, chilled 2 hours, or frozen in individual serving dishes.

Curried Crab Custards
Scallion Brown Rice
Sesame-Cauliflower Salad

Serve individual bowls of crab custard, hot from the oven, with brown rice mixed with chopped scallions and almonds. The side salad of crisp-tender cauliflower is topped with a toasted sesame-seed dressing.

Custard may sound complicated to make, but it is actually very simple. Always bake a custard in a container set in a pan of water; this keeps it from overheating and becoming lumpy or curdled. Remove it from the oven when a knife blade inserted near the edge comes out clean. There will be enough retained heat to firm the center of the custard completely before serving.

Soy sauce and Oriental sesame oil season the chilled cauliflower salad. Light soy, specified here, is usually used in delicately flavored dishes because it is milder and less salty than the "black" or "thick" soy sauces. Aromatic Oriental sesame oil is made from toasted sesame seeds. Use a dark amber-colored Chinese or Japanese brand.

WHAT TO DRINK

A fruity white wine, moderately chilled, will complement this menu. The first choice would be an Italian Chardonnay.

SHOPPING LIST AND STAPLES

¾ pound fresh or "fresh-canned" crabmeat, or two 6-ounce packages frozen
Medium-size cauliflower
Medium-size head butter lettuce, or large bunch watercress
Small bunch scallions
Medium-size bunch parsley
4 large eggs
½ pint heavy cream
½ pint sour cream
4 tablespoons unsalted butter
2½ cups chicken stock, preferably homemade (see page 13), or canned
⅓ cup light vegetable oil
2 tablespoons Oriental sesame oil
¼ to ½ cup light soy sauce
1¼ cups brown rice
2½-ounce bag blanched almonds
2½-ounce package sesame seeds
1 teaspoon curry powder
Salt and freshly ground white pepper

UTENSILS

Small heavy-gauge skillet

Medium-size saucepan with cover
2 small saucepans
Vegetable steamer
13 x 9-inch baking pan
9 x 7-inch baking sheet
Four 1-cup ramekins
2 medium-size bowls
Small bowl
Colander
Salad spinner (optional)
Measuring cups and spoons
Chef's knife
Paring knife
Wooden spoon
Fork
Rubber spatula
Whisk

START-TO-FINISH STEPS

1. Follow crab recipe step 1.
2. Wash parsley, dry with paper towels, and chop enough for rice recipe and for crab recipe; reserve 4 sprigs for garnish, if desired, for crab recipe. Wash and trim scallions, dry with paper towels, chop enough for rice recipe, and mince enough for crab recipe.
3. Follow rice recipe step 1.
4. While almonds are toasting, follow salad recipe step 1.
5. Follow rice recipe steps 2 through 5.
6. While rice is cooking, follow crab recipe steps 2 through 7.
7. While rice is still cooking and crab custards are baking, follow salad recipe steps 2 through 5.
8. Follow rice recipe step 6, crab recipe step 8, and salad recipe step 6, and serve.

RECIPES

Curried Crab Custards

2 tablespoons unsalted butter
2 tablespoons minced scallions
1 teaspoon curry powder
1 cup sour cream
1 cup heavy cream
2 tablespoons chopped parsley plus 4 sprigs for garnish
   (optional)
½ teaspoon salt
⅛ teaspoon freshly ground white pepper
¾ pound fresh or "fresh-canned" crabmeat, or two
   6-ounce packages frozen
4 large eggs

1. Preheat oven to 350 degrees.
2. Melt butter in small saucepan and sauté scallions over medium-high heat 4 to 5 minutes, or until golden. Add curry powder and stir 1 to 2 minutes, until thoroughly blended.
3. Remove saucepan from heat and blend in sour cream, heavy cream, chopped parsley, salt, and pepper. Set aside.

4. Flake crabmeat in small bowl. Set 4 tablespoons aside for garnish, if desired.
5. Beat eggs in medium-size bowl until foamy, then stir in scallion-curry mixture and crabmeat.
6. Pour mixture into 4 ramekins and set in baking pan. Pour boiling water around ramekins to depth of 1 inch.
7. Bake 30 to 35 minutes, or until custards are set and lightly browned on top.
8. When ready to serve, garnish each crabmeat custard with 1 tablespoon reserved crabmeat and parsley sprig, if desired.

Scallion Brown Rice

½ cup blanched almonds
2½ cups chicken stock
2 tablespoons unsalted butter
1¼ cups brown rice
½ cup chopped scallions
Salt
½ cup chopped parsley

1. Scatter almonds on baking sheet and toast in 350-degree oven 5 to 8 minutes, until lightly browned. Stir occasionally and watch carefully to prevent burning.
2. Chop almonds coarsely and set aside.
3. Heat chicken stock in small saucepan over medium-high heat.
4. Melt butter in a medium-size saucepan. Add brown rice and stir until thoroughly coated with butter.
5. Add hot chicken stock and scallions to rice. Stir once, cover pan, and turn heat to low. Cook 40 minutes, or until all liquid is absorbed and rice is tender.
6. When ready to serve, fluff rice with fork, season to taste with salt, and gently fold in parsley and almonds.

Sesame-Cauliflower Salad

4 teaspoons sesame seeds
Medium-size cauliflower
⅓ cup light vegetable oil
2 tablespoons Oriental sesame oil
Medium-size head butter lettuce, or large bunch
   watercress
¼ to ½ cup light soy sauce

1. In skillet set over medium heat, toast sesame seeds 1 to 2 minutes, until fragrant and light brown. Shake skillet frequently to keep seeds from burning. Set aside to cool.
2. Cut cauliflower into florets to measure 3 cups. Wash thoroughly and drain.
3. Steam florets 3 to 4 minutes until crisp-tender.
4. Refresh under cold running water, drain, and dry on paper towels. Toss with vegetable oil and sesame oil to coat thoroughly. Refrigerate until ready to serve.
5. Wash lettuce; dry in salad spinner or with paper towels. Arrange on 4 salad plates.
6. When ready to serve, spoon cauliflower over lettuce, sprinkle each portion with 1 to 2 tablespoons soy sauce and 1 teaspoon toasted sesame seeds.

Tomato and Basil Soup
Garden Harvest Frittata
Gruyère Toasts

This bright meal mixes tomatoes and basil in the soup and six vegetables in the frittata.

The main-course *frittata* includes marinated artichoke hearts and a number of fresh vegetables. Since the success of the dish depends on using top-quality vegetables, select them with care, avoiding any that are not firm and brightly colored or that have signs of decay. For the best flavor, use vegetables the same day you buy them.

WHAT TO DRINK

Select a simple white wine that will not overpower the delicate flavors of this menu. An Italian Soave, a California Chenin Blanc, or a French Vouvray are all recommended.

SHOPPING LIST AND STAPLES

6 medium-size ripe tomatoes (about 3 pounds total
  weight)
2 small zucchini (about ¾ pound total weight)
Large red bell pepper
Large green bell pepper
½ pound fresh peas, or 10-ounce package frozen
Small bunch celery
Small yellow onion
Small bunch scallions
Small bunch fresh basil
Small clove garlic
9 large eggs
½ pound Gruyère cheese
6 tablespoons unsalted butter
6-ounce jar marinated artichoke hearts
¼ cup olive oil, plus ¼ cup, approximately
Long loaf French bread
⅛ teaspoon powdered saffron
½ teaspoon thyme
Salt
Freshly ground pepper
½ cup medium-dry sherry

UTENSILS

Large ovenproof skillet with handle
Large saucepan with cover
17 x 11-inch baking sheet
Medium-size bowl
Measuring cups and spoons
Chef's knife
Paring knife
Bread knife

Wooden spoon
Metal spatula
Grater
Whisk

START-TO-FINISH STEPS

One hour ahead: If using frozen peas for frittata recipe, set out to thaw.

1. Follow soup recipe steps 1 through 5.
2. While soup is simmering, follow frittata recipe steps 1 through 9.
3. Follow toasts recipe steps 1 and 2.
4. Follow frittata recipe step 10 and toasts recipe step 3.
5. Follow soup recipe step 6, toasts recipe step 4, and serve with frittata.

RECIPES

Tomato and Basil Soup

Small yellow onion
Small clove garlic
2 stalks celery
Small bunch fresh basil
2 tablespoons unsalted butter
¼ cup olive oil
6 medium-size ripe tomatoes (about 3 pounds
  total weight)
½ cup medium-dry sherry
⅛ teaspoon powdered saffron
2 teaspoons salt
Freshly ground pepper

1. Peel onion and garlic. Chop onion to measure about ½ cup. Mince garlic to measure about 1 teaspoon. Wash celery, dry with paper towels, and peel; chop to measure about 1½ cups. Wash basil, dry with paper towels, and tear off enough leaves to measure ⅓ cup. Refrigerate remainder for another use.
2. Combine butter and olive oil in large saucepan. Sauté onion, garlic, and celery over medium heat, stirring frequently, about 5 minutes, or until onion is soft but not browned.
3. Wash, dry, halve, and seed tomatoes; chop coarsely to measure about 4 cups.
4. Add tomatoes, basil leaves, sherry, ½ cup water, saffron, salt, and pepper to taste to saucepan.

5. Bring soup to a boil over medium-high heat. Reduce heat and simmer, partially covered, about 30 minutes.
6. Divide among 4 soup bowls and serve immediately.

Garden Harvest Frittata

6-ounce jar marinated artichoke hearts
¼ cup olive oil, approximately
2 small zucchini (about ¾ pound total weight)
Large red bell pepper
Large green bell pepper
Small bunch scallions
½ pound fresh peas, or 10-ounce package frozen
9 large eggs
1 teaspoon salt
Freshly ground pepper
½ teaspoon thyme

1. Preheat oven to 450 degrees.
2. Drain artichoke hearts, reserving marinade in measuring cup; add olive oil to marinade to measure total of ½ cup. Set hearts aside.
3. Pour marinade-oil mixture into skillet with ovenproof handles. Place in oven about 5 minutes, or until mixture begins to bubble.
4. Wash zucchini and dry with paper towels. Cut into ⅛-inch-thick rounds to measure about 2½ cups. Wash red and green bell peppers and dry; halve, seed, remove membranes, and chop to measure about 1¼ cups each.
5. Add zucchini and peppers to hot marinade-oil mixture, tossing to coat. Bake 10 minutes.
6. Trim scallions; chop to measure ½ cup. If using fresh peas, shell to measure ½ cup; if frozen, measure ½ cup and refrigerate remainder for another use.
7. Beat eggs with salt and pepper to taste until foamy.
8. Add artichoke hearts, peas, scallions, and thyme to zucchini mixture. Stir to combine and pour eggs over all.
9. Bake 15 to 20 minutes, or until golden brown and set.
10. Remove frittata from oven and turn on broiler.

Gruyère Toasts

½ pound Gruyère cheese
Long loaf French bread
4 tablespoons unsalted butter
2 teaspoons freshly ground pepper, approximately

1. Grate enough cheese to measure 2 cups.
2. Slice bread in half lengthwise. Butter cut sides.

Coarsely grind about 1 teaspoon pepper over each half and sprinkle with cheese. Place bread on baking sheet and set aside.
3. Set broiler rack 4 inches from heat and broil bread about 5 minutes, or until golden and bubbly.
4. Remove bread from broiler, cut crosswise into 2-inch slices, and serve.

ADDED TOUCH

Use apples in season to give this dish the best texture and flavor. Granny Smiths (usually imported from the Southern hemisphere) are best from July to March, and Newtown Pippins (an old American variety popular in the West) from October to May.

Fried Apples in Brandy with Crème Fraîche

3 medium-size Granny Smith or Newtown Pippin apples
4 tablespoons unsalted butter
½ teaspoon ground cinnamon
1 tablespoon packed dark brown sugar
1 tablespoon brandy
1½ cups crème fraîche (see following recipe)

1. Wash apples; halve, core, seed, and cut into 1-inch chunks.
2. Melt butter in large skillet over medium heat.
3. Add apples to butter, sprinkle with cinnamon and sugar, and sauté over low heat, stirring constantly, about 5 to 7 minutes, until tender.
4. Turn heat to high. Add brandy and stir about 2 minutes, until sugar mixture becomes sticky.
5. Spoon into serving dishes and serve warm or cool, topped with crème fraîche.

Crème Fraîche

4 tablespoons buttermilk or 1 cup sour cream
2 cups heavy cream

1. In a heavy-gauge saucepan, combine the buttermilk or sour cream with the heavy cream. Heat over low heat just until the chill is removed and the mixture feels tepid to your finger (about 85 degrees).
2. Pour mixture into a glass jar and let stand at room temperature (ideally 75 degrees but no hotter than 85 degrees). It will thicken after about 6 to 8 hours.
3. When mixture is thick, stir, cover the jar, and refrigerate. The crème fraîche will last up to 10 days.

Acknowledgments

Special thanks to the American Egg Board for their assistance in the preparation of this volume.

The Editors would like to thank the following for their courtesy in lending items for photography: *Cover:* fork—Gorham; plates—Columbus Avenue General Store; tablecloth, napkin—Conran's. *Frontispiece:* whisk—Charles Lamalle. *Pages 18–19:* fork—Gorham; tablecloth—Conran's; dishes, napkin—Ad Hoc Softwares. *Pages 22–23:* flatware—Gorham; napkins, rug—Museum of American Folk Art Shop. *Page 25:* flatware—Gorham; napkin, mat, plate—Columbus Avenue General Store. *Pages 28–29:* flatware—Gorham; glasses—Pottery Barn; tablecloth—Conran's; dishes, napkins—Frank McIntosh at Henri Bendel. *Page 32:* plate—Pottery Barn; mat, napkin—Frank McIntosh at Henri Bendel. *Page 34:* fork—Gorham; napkin—Leacock & Co.; tablecloth—Conran's; dishes—Dan Bleier. *pages 36–37:* plates—Claudia Shwide; countertop—Formica® Brand Laminate by Formica Corp. *Page 40:* server—Gorham; dishes, glasses—Haviland & Co. *Page 43:* flatware—Gorham; napkin—Ad Hoc Softwares; dishes—Buffalo China; tiles—Amaru Tile. *Pages 46–47:* tiles—Terra Design, Inc., Morristown, NJ; glasses—Conran's; napkin—The Lauffer Co. *Page 50:* glasses—Wolfman-Gold & Good Co.; platter—Claudia Shwide; napkins—Ad Hoc Softwares. *Pages 53:* forks—Gorham; tablecloth—Laura Ashley. *Pages 56–57:* napkins—Leacock & Co.; linens—Ad Hoc Softwares; service plates—Conran's; dishes—Broadway Panhandler. *Page 60:* flatware—Gorham; dishes, mat, glass—Ad Hoc Housewares; napkin—Ad Hoc Softwares. *Page 63:* napkin—Leacock & Co.; rug—Bowl & Board. *Pages 66–67:* plate—Ad Hoc Housewares; glass—Gorham; napkin—Leacock & Co. *Pages 70–71:* dishes—Dan Bleier; rug—Conran's. *Page 73:* flatware—Gorham; dishes—Dan Bleier; tablecloth—Conran's; napkin—Leacock & Co. *Pages 76–77:* flatware, glass—Gorham; plates—Dan Levy. *Page 80:* flatware, glasses—Gorham; dishes—Dorothy Hafner; tablecloth—Conran's. *Page 82:* flatware—Wallace Silversmiths; dishes—Mad Monk. *Pages 84–85:* server—Wallace Silversmiths; bowl—Kosta Boda; basket—Urban Outfitters; pie plate—Pottery Barn; linens—China Seas. *Pages 88–89:* tablecloth—Wolfman-Gold & Good Co.; plates—Claudia Shwide. *Page 91:* basket—Be Seated; glass bowl, platter—Rörstrand; napkins—Urban Outfitters; tablecloth—Conran's. *Pages 94–95:* servers, platters, bowls—Pottery Barn. *Page 98:* plate—Bennington Pottery; napkin—Leacock & Co.; small plate, ramekin—Mark Anderson; countertop—Formica® Brand Laminate by Formica Corp. *Page 100:* dishes—Dorothy Hafner. *Kitchen equipment courtesy of:* White-Westinghouse, Commercial Aluminum Cookware Co., Robot-Coupe, Caloric, Kitchen-Aid, J.A. Henckels Zwillingswerk, Inc., Rubbermaid, Tappan, Litton Microwave Cooking, Schwabel Corp., Farberware. Illustrations by Ray Skibinski Production by Giga Communications

Index

*Time-Life Books Inc. offers a wide
range of fine recordings, including
a Big Band series. For subscription
information, call 1-800-621-7026, or
write* TIME-LIFE MUSIC, *Time & Life
Building, Chicago, Illinois 60611.*

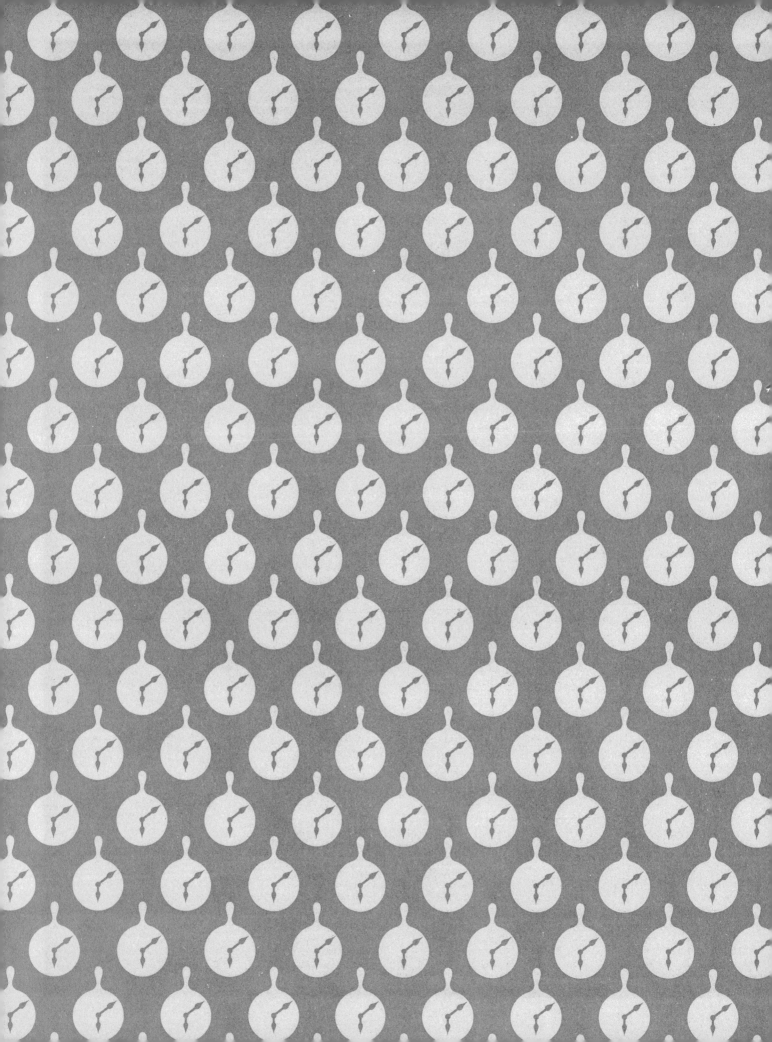